COOKSHELF

Fish &
Seafood

Carol Tennant

This is a Parragon Publishing Book
This edition published in 2004

Parragon Publishing
Queen Street House
4 Queen Street
Bath BA1 1HE, UK

ISBN: 0-75255-477-8

Printed in China

Note
Cup measurements in this book are for American cups. This book also uses imperial and metric measurements.
Follow the same units of measurement throughout; do not mix metric and imperial.
All spoon measurements are level: teaspoons are assumed to be 5 ml and tablespoons are assumed to be 15 ml.
Unless otherwise stated, milk is assumed to be full-fat, eggs and individual vegetables
such as potatoes are medium, and pepper is freshly ground black pepper.

Recipes using uncooked eggs should be
avoided by infants, the elderly, pregnant women, and anyone
suffering from an illness.

Contents

Introduction

Seafood rightly deserves its image as a healthy food. It is high in protein and with the added bonus of oily fish, such as mackerel and herring, being high in polyunsaturated fat—this is the one that helps reduce cholesterol levels. White fish are a good source of minerals as well as being low in fat, especially if poached, steamed, or lightly grilled. Although shellfish have been linked with high cholesterol, they are also low in saturated fats and are therefore fine eaten in moderation. The sheer variety of fish and shellfish is staggering. If you decided to eat seafood just once a week, you could go for a whole year without eating the same dish twice. Seafood is also quick and easy to prepare, making it an attractive ingredient to the busy cook. Often sold ready-to-cook, fish can be prepared in minutes and most shellfish is sold already cooked, needing even less preparation.

Fish is also very good value for money compared to meat, as there is much less waste and no fat or gristle to contend with. Therefore making fish a regular part of your diet makes a lot of sense.

BUYING FISH AND SHELLFISH

Wherever you are shopping for fish, at your local trusted fish market or supermarket, the guidelines are the same:

• The eyes of the fish should be clear, bright, and moist. Fish with dull, gray, or cloudy eyes should be avoided.

• The gills of the fish should be bright red or pink, not dull and not gray.

• The fish should smell of the sea and nothing else.

• If you press the fish lightly with your thumb, the flesh should spring back, leaving little or no imprint.

• The shells of hinged shellfish, such as oysters, mussels, and clams, should be tightly closed prior to cooking. If they are slightly open, tap them sharply. If they do not close, discard them.

• Cooked shellfish should smell fresh, with no hint of ammonia. If available, check the expiration date.

STORING

As you never know how long ago the fish was caught, especially in a supermarket, it is best to buy fish and cook it on the same day. Unfortunately, modern refrigerators are not ideal places to store fish as they tend to have a temperature of about 38°F and fish is best kept at 32°F. If you have to keep fish, don't keep it for more than one or two days. Put the fish into a plastic container and scatter over some ice. Cover with plastic wrap and keep in the coldest part of the refrigerator.

Firmer fleshed fish, such as turbot, Dover sole, and monkfish, freeze better than less firm-fleshed fish like bass, lemon sole, and flounder but all will deteriorate over a relatively short period. Oily fish is the least successful when frozen. However, if you have to keep your fish for more than a day or two, then freezing is the best option. Ensure that you thaw fish thoroughly and slowly before cooking.

PREPARATION

How much preparation your fish needs depends on where you buy it. Supermarkets may have a wet fish counter with a trained butcher on hand while others sell their fish prepacked on styrofoam trays. Many fish are sold already scaled and gutted, and are often available either whole or filleted. It is usually cheaper, however, to buy a whole fish and prepare it yourself. Local fishermen will usually do this job for you for the price of a whole fish. However, it is not difficult to do yourself and only takes a bit of practice.

EQUIPMENT

Although, in general, you don't need a great deal of specialized equipment, there are a few items you might consider if you plan on cooking a lot of fish. If, for example, you are planning on poaching whole fish, then a wise investment would be a fish poacher. This is an oblong stainless steel pan with a lifter and lid. They usually come in several sizes.

A wok or large, heavy-based frying pan is useful for frying and stir-frying. If you like to steam fish you might like to consider a double boiler, bamboo steamer, or electric steamer . A thermometer is useful for deep-frying as is a deep-frying basket and large pan.

If you intend cleaning your own fish, a good filleting knife is a must. Tweezers are also useful for removing small bones. Different fish suit different cooking methods but, as a general rule, poaching, steaming, and stewing tend to produce moister results than grilling, baking, or barbecuing. Drying out can be minimized, however, if the latter three methods are used at sufficiently high temperatures to reduce moisture loss by cooking the fish very quickly.

COOKING METHODS

POACHING
The fish is immersed in a poaching liquid, which might be a court-bouillon, fish stock, milk, beer, or cider. Bring the liquid to a boil and as soon as it boils, remove the pan from the heat and leave the fish to finish cooking in the residual heat. This method helps to prevent overcooking and is also excellent if you want to serve the fish cold.

STEAMING
Both fish and shellfish benefit from being steamed. Again, a flavored liquid can be used for the steaming, which will impart some of its flavor to the fish as it is being cooked. This method is especially good for keeping the fish moist and the flavor delicate. Steaming can be done in a fish poacher, double boiler, or steamer inserted over a pan of boiling water.

STEWING
Either whole fish or smaller pieces can be cooked in liquid along with other ingredients, such as vegetables, as a stew. The fish flavors the liquid as it cooks, giving a distinctive flavor.

GRILLING/BROILING
This is one of the quickest and easiest cooking methods for fish. Cook either whole fish, steaks, or fillets. Shellfish can also be grilled, but you may need to halve them lengthwise first. Whatever you are cooking, ensure that the broiler is on its highest setting and that the fish is cooked as close to the heat source as possible. A barbecue is also a very useful tool for grilling fish. Brush the fish with butter, oil, or a marinade before and during cooking to ensure that the flesh remains moist.

BAKING AND ROASTING
This covers all methods of cooking in the oven, including open roasting, casseroling, or en papillote. This is a good method to choose for entertaining because, once the dish is in the oven, you are then free to attend to other things.

DEEP-FRYING
The fish is either coated in batter, flour, or breadcrumbs and deep fried in oil. You need a large, heavy-based saucepan or a deep fat fryer. Large pieces of fish in batter are best cooked at a lower temperature of 350° F which allows the fish to cook without burning the batter. Smaller pieces of fish, like goujons in breadcrumbs, should be cooked at a higher temperature of 375° F. Drain deep-fried items well on paper towel to ensure that they remain crisp.

PAN-FRYING
This is a quick method for cooking fish and shellfish and can take as little as 3–4 minutes. A shallow layer of oil or butter and oil is heated in a frying pan, the fish is added and cooked until just tender and lightly browned. A good nonstick frying pan is an essential piece of equipment.

The argument for increasing the amount of fish and seafood in our diets is compelling. Fish and seafood can provide variety, versatility, creativity, and luxury as well as being much more healthy than meat. Why not give it a try?

Snacks & Appetizers

The dishes in this chapter are designed either as appetizers for the main course to come or as snacks to serve with drinks. Fish and seafood make excellent starters as they are full of flavor and can be turned into a variety of delicious dishes. Fish is also much lighter than meat and won't be too filling.

Fish cooks quickly, making it ideal for entertaining. Many of the dishes in this chapter can be prepared in advance and served cold, such as the Anchovy Bites, the Smoked Mackerel Pâté, and the Lime & Basil Cured Salmon, or simply reheated, like the Curried Mussel Tartlets or the Stuffed Squid.

There is also a good selection of first course options, for example the Thai Crab Omelette, Potted Shrimps, and Maryland Crab Cakes with Basil & Tomato Dressing, and lots of lovely salad ideas, including the Smoked Haddock Salad and the Bruschetta with Anchoiade, Mixed Tomatoes & Mozzarella.

Anchovy Bites

Makes: about 30

INGREDIENTS

1½ cups all-purpose flour
6 tbsp. butter, cut into
    small pieces
4 tbsp. freshly grated
    Parmesan cheese
3 tbsp. Dijon mustard
salt and pepper

ANCHOIADE
2 x 1¾ oz. cans anchovy fillets in
    olive oil, drained
scant/½ cup milk
2 garlic cloves, roughly chopped
1 tbsp. roughly chopped fresh
    flat-leaf parsley

1 tbsp. roughly chopped
    fresh basil
1 tbsp. lemon juice
2 tbsp. blanched almonds,
    toasted and roughly chopped
4 tbsp. olive oil

1 To make the pastry, sift the flour into a large bowl and add the butter. Rub together until the mixture resembles breadcrumbs. Stir in half the Parmesan cheese and salt. Add enough cold water (about 3 tbsp.) to form a firm dough. Knead briefly, wrap in plastic wrap and refrigerate for 30 minutes.

2 Meanwhile, make the anchoiade. Put the drained anchovies into a small bowl and pour over the milk to cover. Leave to soak for 10 minutes. Drain the anchovies and pat dry on paper towels. Discard the milk.

3 Roughly chop the anchovies and put into a food processor or blender with the garlic, parsley, basil, lemon juice, almonds and 2 tablespoons of the oil. Blend until smooth. Scrape out of the food processor or blender and stir in the remaining olive oil and pepper to taste.

4 Remove the pastry from the refrigerator and roll out very thinly to a rectangle measuring 20 x 15 in. Spread thinly with 2 tbsp. of the anchoiade and the Dijon mustard. Sprinkle over the remaining Parmesan cheese and some black pepper.

5 Starting from a long edge, roll up tightly then slice crossways into ½ in. thick slices. Arrange cut-side up and well spaced on a nonstick baking sheet.

6 Place in a preheated oven at 400° F for 20 minutes until golden. Cool on a wire rack.

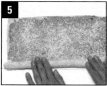

Bruschetta with Anchoiade, Mixed Tomatoes & Mozzarella

Serves 4

INGREDIENTS

2 x 5½ oz. balls buffalo
    mozzarella, drained
1 cup orange cherry tomatoes
1 cup red cherry tomatoes
2 ripe plum or red beefsteak
    tomatoes

2 ripe orange or yellow beefsteak
    tomatoes
4 tbsp. extra-virgin olive oil, plus
    extra for drizzling
1 tbsp. balsamic vinegar
8 thick slices ciabatta or other
    rustic country bread

1 garlic clove
4 tbsp. anchoiade (see Anchovy
    Bites, page 8)
handful basil leaves
salt and pepper

1 Slice the mozzarella balls into thick slices. Set aside. Halve the cherry tomatoes and thickly slice the plum and beefsteak tomatoes.

2 To make the dressing, whisk together the olive oil, balsamic vinegar, and salt and pepper.

3 Toast the bread on both sides then rub one side with the garlic clove. Drizzle with a little olive oil. Spread the anchoiade on the toasts.

4 To assemble the salad, arrange the sliced tomatoes on each of 4 serving plates and scatter with cherry tomatoes.

5 Top the toasts with the mozzarella slices and 2–3 halved cherry tomatoes. Cook under a preheated broiler for 3–4 minutes until softened. Drizzle over the dressing and scatter with basil leaves and black pepper.

6 Put 2 slices of toast on the plates.

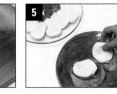

Bagna Cauda with Crudités

Serves 8

INGREDIENTS

1 yellow pepper	1 bunch scallions	1³/₄ oz. can anchovies in oil,
3 stalks celery	2 beets, cooked and peeled	drained and chopped
2 carrots	8 radishes	8 tbsp. butter
½ cauliflower	8 oz. boiled new potatoes	Italian bread, to serve
½ cup mushrooms	1 cup olive oil	
1 bulb. fennel	5 garlic cloves, crushed	

1 Prepare the vegetables. Deseed and slice the pepper thickly. Cut the celery into 3 in. lengths. Cut the carrots into batons. Score the mushrooms as in the photograph. Separate the cauliflower into florets. Cut the fennel in half lengthwise then cut each half into 4 lengthwise. Trim the scallions. Cut the beets into eighths. Trim the radishes. Cut the potatoes in half, if large. Arrange the vegetables on a large serving platter.

2 Heat the oil very gently in a saucepan. Add the garlic and anchovies and cook very gently, stirring, until the anchovies have dissolved. Take care not to brown or burn the garlic.

3 Add the butter and as soon as it has melted, serve straight away with the selection of crudités and plenty of bread.

COOK'S TIP

If you have one, a fondue set is perfect for serving this dish as the sauce can be kept hot at the table.

Giant Garlic Shrimp

Serves 4

INGREDIENTS

1 cup olive oil

4 garlic cloves, finely chopped

2 hot red chilies, deseeded and
finely chopped

1 lb. precooked jumbo shrimp

2 tbsp. chopped fresh flat-leaf
parsley

salt and pepper

crusty bread, to serve

lemon wedges, to garnish

1 Heat the oil in a large frying pan over a low heat. Add the garlic and chilies and cook for 1–2 minutes until softened but not colored.

2 Add the shrimp and stir-fry for 2–3 minutes until heated through and coated in the oil and garlic mixture. Remove from the heat.

3 Add the parsley and stir well to mix. Season with salt and pepper to taste.

4 Divide the shrimp and garlic oil between warmed serving dishes and serve with lots of crusty bread. Garnish with the lemon wedges.

COOK'S TIP

If you can get hold of raw shrimp, cook them as above but increase the cooking time to 5–6 minutes until the shrimp are cooked through and turn bright pink.

Mini Shrimp Spring Rolls

Makes about 30

INGREDIENTS

½ cup dried rice vermicelli
1 carrot, cut into matchsticks
¼ cup snow peas, shredded
    thinly lengthwise
3 scallions, finely chopped
3½ oz. precooked peeled shrimp
2 garlic cloves, crushed

1 tsp. sesame oil
2 tbsp. light soy sauce
1 tsp. chili sauce
7 oz. phyllo pastry, cut into 6 in.
    squares
1 egg white, beaten
vegetable oil, for deep-frying

dark soy sauce, sweet chili sauce,
    or sweet-and-sour dipping
    sauce (see Thai Fish Cakes,
    page 40), for dipping

1 Cook the rice vermicelli according to the package instructions. Drain thoroughly. Roughly chop and set aside. Bring a pan of salted water to a boil and blanch the carrot and snow peas for 1 minute. Drain and refresh under cold water. Drain again and pat dry on paper towels. Mix together with the noodles and add the scallions, shrimp, garlic, sesame oil, soy sauce, and chili sauce. Set aside.

2 Fold the phyllo pastry squares in half diagonally to form triangles. Lay a triangle on the work surface, with the fold facing you, and place a spoonful of the mixture in the center. Roll over the wrapper to enclose the filling, then bring over the corners to enclose the ends of the roll. Brush the point of the spring roll furthest from you with a little beaten egg white and continue rolling to seal. Continue with the remaining phyllo triangles to make about 30 spring rolls.

3 Fill a deep fat fryer or saucepan about a third full with vegetable oil and heat to 375° F or until a cube of bread browns in 30 seconds. Fry the spring rolls, 4 or 5 at a time, for 1–2 minutes or until golden and crisp. Drain on paper towels. Fry the remaining spring rolls in batches.

4 Serve them hot with dark soy sauce, sweet chili sauce, or sweet-and-sour sauce for dipping.

Shrimp Satay

Serves 4

INGREDIENTS

12 peeled raw jumbo shrimp

MARINADE
1 tsp. ground coriander
1 tsp. ground cumin
2 tbsp. light soy sauce
4 tbsp. vegetable oil
1 tbsp. curry powder
1 tbsp. ground turmeric

½ cup coconut milk
3 tbsp. sugar

PEANUT SAUCE
2 tbsp. vegetable oil
3 garlic cloves, crushed
1 tbsp. red curry paste (see Red
   Shrimp Curry, page 102)
½ cup coconut milk

1 cup fish or chicken stock
1 tbsp. sugar
1 tsp. salt
1 tbsp. lemon juice
4 tbsp. unsalted roasted peanuts,
   finely chopped
4 tbsp. dried breadcrumbs

1 Slit the shrimp down their backs and remove the black vein, if any. Set aside. Mix together the marinade ingredients and add the shrimp. Mix together well, cover and set aside for at least 8 hours or overnight.

2 To make the peanut sauce, heat the oil in a large frying pan until very hot. Add the garlic and fry until just starting to color. Add the curry paste and mix together well, cooking for an additional 30 seconds. Add the coconut milk, stock, sugar, salt and lemon juice and stir well. Boil for 1–2 minutes, stirring constantly. Add the peanuts and breadcrumbs and mix together well. Pour the sauce into a bowl and set aside.

3 Using 4 skewers, thread 3 shrimp on to each. Cook under a preheated hot broiler or on the barbecue for 3–4 minutes on each side until just cooked through. Serve immediately with the peanut sauce.

Potted Shrimp

Serves 4

INGREDIENTS

1¼ cups unsalted butter	pinch cayenne pepper	salt and pepper
14 oz. brown shrimp in their	½ tsp. ground mace	brown bread, to serve
shells or 8 oz. cooked	1 garlic clove, crushed	lemon wedges and fresh parsley
peeled shrimp	1 tbsp. chopped fresh parsley	sprigs, to garnish

---

1 Heat the butter in a small saucepan until melted and foaming. Set aside for 10 minutes or until the butter separates. Carefully skim off the clear yellow liquid and discard the white milk solids. The clear yellow oil remaining is clarified butter.

2 Peel the shrimp, discarding the shells. Heat 2 tablespoons of the clarified butter in a frying pan and add the shrimp. Stir in the cayenne, mace, and garlic. Increase the heat and stir-fry for 30 seconds until very hot. Remove from the heat, stir in the parsley and season to taste.

3 Divide the shrimp between 4 small ramekins, pressing down with the back of a spoon. Pour over the remaining clarified butter to cover. Refrigerate until the butter has set.

4 Remove the ramekins from the refrigerator 30 minutes before serving to allow the butter to soften. Toast the brown bread and serve with the shrimp, garnished with lemon wedges and fresh parsley sprigs if desired.

COOK'S TIP

The most authentic shrimp to use for this recipe are the tiny brown shrimp. They have a full flavor and soak up the butter well. If your fish market can't supply them, substitute the pink peeled variety.

Prunes Stuffed with Mussels

Makes 24

INGREDIENTS

3 tbsp. port
1 tbsp. clear honey
2 cloves garlic, crushed

24 large stoned prunes
24 live mussels

12 slices of bacon
salt and pepper

1 Mix together the port, honey and garlic then season. Put the prunes into a small bowl and pour over the port mixture. Cover and leave to marinate for at least 4 hours and preferably overnight.

2 Next day, clean the mussels by scrubbing or scraping the shells and pulling out any beards. Put the mussels in a large saucepan with just the water that clings to their shells. Cook, covered, over a high heat for 3–4 minutes until all the mussels have opened. Discard any mussels that remain closed.

3 Drain the mussels, reserving the cooking liquid. Allow to cool then remove the mussels from their shells.

4 Using the back of a knife, stretch the bacon slices then cut in half widthwise. Lift the prunes from their marinade, reserving any that remains.

5 Stuff each prune with a mussel then wrap with a piece of bacon. Secure with a toothpick. Repeat to make 24.

6 In a saucepan, simmer together the mussel cooking liquid and remaining marinade until reduced and syrupy. Brush the stuffed prunes with this mixture. Place under a preheated hot broiler and cook for 3–4 minutes each side, turning regularly and brushing with the marinade, until the bacon is crisp and golden. Serve while still hot.

VARIATION

As an alternative to smoked bacon use pancetta or Parma ham, cut into strips, instead and cook as above.

Mussel Fritters

Serves 4–6

INGREDIENTS

1½ cups all-purpose flour
pinch of salt
1 egg
1 cup lager beer of your choice
2 lb. live mussels
vegetable oil, for deep-frying

GARLIC AND HERB MAYONNAISE
1 egg yolk
1 tsp. Dijon mustard
1 tsp. white wine vinegar
2 tbsp. chopped fresh mixed
    herbs, such as parsley,
    chives, basil, thyme

2 garlic cloves, crushed
1 cup olive oil
salt and pepper

TO GARNISH
lemon slices
fresh parsley

1 To make the batter, put the flour into the bowl with a pinch of salt. Add the egg and half the lager and whisk until smooth. Gradually add the remaining lager, whisking until smooth. Set aside for 30 minutes.

2 Clean the mussels by scrubbing or scraping the shells and pulling out any beards that are attached to them. Discard any with broken shells or any that refuse to close when tapped. Put the mussels into a large pan with just the water on their shells and cook, covered, over a high heat for 3–4 minutes, shaking the pan occasionally, until all the mussels have opened. Discard any mussels that remain closed. Drain and set aside until cool enough to handle, then remove the mussels from their shells.

3 To make the garlic and herb mayonnaise, in a food processor or blender, whisk together the egg yolk, mustard, vinegar, herbs, garlic, and seasoning until frothy. Keep the machine running, and add the olive oil, drop by drop to begin with, until the mixture begins to thicken. Continue adding the oil in a steady stream. Season and add a little hot water if the mixture seems too thick. Set aside.

4 Meanwhile, fill a deep saucepan about a third full with vegetable oil and heat to 375° F or until a cube of bread browns in 30 seconds. Drop the mussels, a few at a time, into the batter and lift out with a slotted spoon. Drop into the hot oil and cook for 1–2 minutes until the batter is crisp and golden. Drain on paper towels. Serve hot with the garlic and herb mayonnaise garnished with lemon slices.

Mussels with Pesto

Serves 4

INGREDIENTS

2 lb. live mussels
6 tbsp. chopped fresh basil
2 garlic cloves, crushed
1 tbsp. pine nuts, toasted

2 tbsp. freshly grated Parmesan
   cheese
scant ½ cup olive oil
2 cups fresh white breadcrumbs
salt and pepper

TO GARNISH
basil leaves
tomato slices

1 Clean the mussels by scrubbing or scraping the shells and pulling out any beards that are attached to them. Discard any with broken shells or any that refuse to close when tapped. Put the mussels into a large pan with just the water on their shells and cook, covered, over a high heat for 3–4 minutes, shaking the pan occasionally, until all the mussels have opened. Discard any mussels that remain closed. Drain, reserving the cooking liquid, and set aside until cool enough to handle.

2 Strain the cooking liquid into a clean pan and simmer until reduced to about 1 tablespoon. Put the liquid into a food processor with the basil, garlic, pine nuts and Parmesan and process until finely chopped. Add the olive oil and breadcrumbs and process until well mixed.

3 Open the mussels and loosen from their shells, discarding the empty half of the shell. Divide the pesto breadcrumbs between the cooked mussels.

4 Cook under a preheated broiler until the breadcrumbs are crisp, golden and the mussels heated through. Serve immediately with slices of tomato and garnish with basil leaves.

VARIATION

If you want an alternative to pine nuts add 3 oz. roughly chopped, drained sun-dried tomatoes in oil to the pesto instead.

Curried Mussel Tartlets

Serves 6

INGREDIENTS

1½ cups all-purpose flour	CURRIED MUSSEL FILLING	¾ cup heavy cream
½ tsp. turmeric	1 lb. live mussels	2 egg yolks
½ tsp. salt	2 tsp. vegetable oil	2 tbsp. chopped cilantro
6 tbsp. butter, diced	2 garlic cloves, finely chopped	salt and pepper
1 oz. finely chopped walnuts	1 tsp. grated ginger root	
salad, to serve	1 tsp. mild curry paste	

1 To make the pastry, sift the flour, turmeric, and salt into the bowl of a food processor or large bowl. Add the butter and process, or rub in with your fingers, until the mixture resembles fine breadcrumbs. Stir in the walnuts and add 2 tablespoons cold water. Process or mix briefly until the dough starts to come together, adding a little more water if necessary. Do not overprocess. Turn the dough onto a lightly floured surface and knead briefly until smooth. Wrap in plastic wrap and leave to rest in the refrigerator for 30 minutes.

2 Clean the mussels by scrubbing or scraping the shells and pulling out any beards that are attached to them. Discard any with broken shells or any that refuse to close when tapped. Put the mussels into a large pan with just the water on their shells and cook, covered, over a high heat for 3–4 minutes, shaking the pan occasionally, until all the mussels have opened. Discard any mussels that remain closed, drain and set aside until cool enough to handle. Remove the mussels from their shells.

3 Heat the oil in a small frying pan, add the garlic and ginger. Stir-fry for 1 minute before stirring in the curry paste and mixing well. Remove from the heat and add the cream. Set aside and allow to cool.

4 Divide the pastry into 6 equal pieces. Roll out each piece thinly and use to line 3½ in. individual tartlet tins. Carefully line the pastry with foil and fill with baking beans. Place in a preheated oven, at 400° F, for 10 minutes. Remove the foil and beans and cook for an additional 5 minutes. Remove from the oven and allow to cool slightly. Reduce oven temperature to 350° F.

5 Divide the cooked mussels between the cooled pastry cases. Whisk the egg yolks and cilantro into the cooled cream mixture. Then season and pour the mixture into the pastry cases to cover the mussels. Bake in the preheated oven for 25 minutes until the filling has just set and the pastry is golden. Allow to cool and serve warm with salad.

Calamari

Serves 4

INGREDIENTS

1 cup all-purpose flour
1 tsp. salt
2 eggs

¾ cup soda water
1 lb. prepared squid (see method),
    cut into rings

vegetable oil, for deep-frying
lemon wedges, to serve
parsley sprigs, to garnish

---

1 Sift the flour into a bowl with the salt. Add the eggs and half the soda water and whisk together until smooth. Gradually whisk in the remaining soda water until the batter is smooth. Set aside.

2 To prepare whole squid, hold the body firmly and grasp the tentacles just inside the body. Pull firmly to remove the innards. Find the transparent "backbone" and remove. Grasp the wings on the outside of the body and pull to remove the outer skin. Trim the tentacles just below the beak and reserve.

3 Wash the body and tentacles under running water. Slice the body across into ½ in. rings. Drain well on paper towels.

4 Meanwhile, fill a deep saucepan about a third full with vegetable oil and heat to 375° F or until a cube of bread browns in 30 seconds.

5 Dip the squid rings and tentacles into the batter, a few at a time, and drop into the hot oil. Fry for 1–2 minutes until crisp and golden. Drain on paper towels. Cook all the squid this way. Serve immediately while still hot with garnished with lemon wedges and parsley sprigs.

COOK'S TIP

If you don't like the idea of cleaning squid yourself, get your fish market to do it. Sometimes, squid is even sold already cut into rings. Alternatively, you could use prepared baby squid for this dish.

Stuffed Squid

Serves 4

INGREDIENTS

12 baby squid, cleaned	1 tbsp. seedless raisins	¼ cup sun-dried tomatoes in oil,
1 tsp. salt	1 tbsp. pine nuts, toasted	drained and finely chopped
4 tbsp. olive oil	1 tbsp. chopped fresh flat-leaf	½ cup dry white wine
1 small onion, finely chopped	parsley	salt and pepper
1 garlic clove, finely chopped	14 oz. can chopped tomatoes	crusty bread, to serve
1 cup basmati rice		

1 Separate the tentacles from the body of the squid. Chop the tentacles and set aside. Rub the squid tubes inside and out with the salt and set aside while you prepare the stuffing.

2 Heat 1 tablespoon of the olive oil in a frying pan and add the onion and garlic. Cook for 4–5 minutes until softened and lightly browned. Add the chopped tentacles and fry for 2–3 minutes. Add the rice, raisins, pine nuts, and parsley and seasoning. Remove from the heat.

3 Allow the rice mixture to cool slightly and spoon it into the squid tubes, about three quarters full to allow the rice to expand. You may need to open the squid tubes a little by making a small cut. Secure each filled squid with a toothpick.

4 Heat the remaining oil in a large flameproof casserole. Add the squid and fry for a few minutes on all sides until lightly browned. Add the tomatoes, sun-dried tomatoes, wine and seasoning. Bake in a preheated oven at 350° F, for 45 minutes. Serve hot or cold with plenty of crusty bread.

COOK'S TIP

If you have difficulty finding baby squid, larger ones work very well and the cooking time is the same. Use cleaned squid weighing 8 oz. in total for the amount of stuffing in this recipe.

Tempura Smelt

Serves 4

INGREDIENTS

1 lb. smelt, thawed if frozen	CHILI AND LIME MAYONNAISE
¾ cup all-purpose flour	1 egg yolk
½ cup cornstarch	1 tbsp. lime juice
½ tsp. salt	1 fresh red chili, deseeded and
1 cup cold water	finely chopped
1 egg	2 tbsp. chopped cilantro
a few ice cubes	1 cup light olive oil
vegetable oil, for deep-frying	salt and pepper

1 To make the mayonnaise, in the bowl of a food processor or blender, mix together the egg yolk, lime juice, chili, cilantro, and seasoning until foaming. With the machine running, gradually add the olive oil, drop by drop to begin with, until the mixture begins to thicken. Continue adding the oil in a steady stream. Adjust seasoning and add a little hot water if the mixture seems too thick. Put to one side.

2 For the tempura smelt, wash and dry the fish. Set aside on paper towels. In a large bowl, sift together the flour, cornstarch, and salt. Whisk together the water, egg, and ice cubes and pour on to the flour. Whisk briefly until the mixture is runny, but still lumpy with dry bits of flour still apparent.

3 Meanwhile, fill a deep saucepan about a third full with vegetable oil and heat to 375° F or until a cube of bread browns in 30 seconds.

4 Dip the smelt, a few at a time, into the batter and carefully drop into the hot oil. Fry for 1 minute until the batter is crisp but not browned. Drain on paper towels. Cook all the smelt this way. Serve hot with the chili and lime mayonnaise.

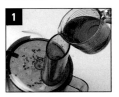

Smoked Mackerel Pâté

Serves 4

INGREDIENTS

7 oz. smoked mackerel fillet
1 small, hot green chili, deseeded
    and chopped
1 garlic clove, chopped
3 tbsp. cilantro leaves

⅔ cup sour cream
1 small red onion, chopped
2 tbsp. lime juice
salt and pepper

MELBA TOAST
4 slices white bread, crusts
    removed

1 Skin and flake the mackerel fillet, removing any small bones. Put the flesh in the bowl of a food processor along with the chili, garlic, cilantro, and sour cream. Blend until smooth.

2 Transfer the mixture to a bowl and mix in the onion and lime juice. Season to taste. The pâté will seem very soft at this stage but will firm up in the refrigerator. Refrigerate for several hours or overnight if possible.

3 To make the melba toasts, place the trimmed bread slices under a preheated medium broiler and toast lightly on both sides. Split the toasts in half horizontally, then cut each across diagonally to form 4 triangles per slice.

4 Put the triangles, untoasted side up, under the broiler and toast until golden and curled at the edges. Serve warm or cold with the mackerel pâté.

COOK'S TIP

This pâté is also very good served with crudités.

Smoked Haddock Salad

Serves 4

INGREDIENTS

350 g/12 oz. smoked
    haddock fillet
4 tbsp. olive oil
1 tbsp. lemon juice
2 tbsp. sour cream

1 tbsp. hot water
2 tbsp. chopped fresh chives
1 plum tomato, peeled, deseeded
    and diced
8 quail's eggs

4 thick slices multigrain bread
4 oz. mixed salad leaves
chives, to garnish
salt and pepper

1 Fill a large frying pan with water and bring to a boil. Add the smoked haddock fillet, cover and remove from the heat. Leave for 10 minutes until the fish is tender. Lift from the poaching water, drain and leave until cool enough to handle. Flake the flesh, removing any small bones. Set aside. Discard the poaching water.

2 Whisk together the olive oil, lemon juice, sour cream, hot water, chives and seasoning. Stir in the tomato. Set aside.

3 Bring a small saucepan of water to a boil. Carefully lower the quail's eggs into the water. Cook the eggs for 3–4 minutes from when the water returns to a boil (3 minutes for a slightly soft center, 4 minutes for a firm center). Drain immediately and refresh under cold running water. Carefully peel the eggs, cut in half lengthwise and set aside.

4 Toast the multigrain bread and cut each across diagonally to form 4 triangles. Arrange 2 halves on 4 serving plates. Top with the salad leaves, then the flaked fish and finally the quail's eggs. Spoon over the dressing and garnish with a few extra chives.

COOK'S TIP

When buying smoked haddock, and smoked fish in general, look for undyed fish, which is always superior in quality.

Thai Fish Cakes with Sweet & Sour Chili Dipping Sauce

Serves 4

INGREDIENTS

1 lb. firm white fish, such as hake, haddock, or cod, skinned and roughly chopped
1 tbsp. Thai fish sauce
1 tbsp. red curry paste (see Red Shrimp Curry, page 102)
1 kaffir lime leaf, finely shredded

2 tbsp. chopped cilantro
1 egg
1 tsp. brown sugar
large pinch salt
1½ oz. green beans, thinly sliced crossways
vegetable oil, for pan-frying

SWEET AND SOUR DIPPING SAUCE
4 tbsp. sugar
1 tbsp. cold water
3 tbsp. white rice vinegar
2 small, hot chilies, finely chopped
1 tbsp. fish sauce

1 For the fish cakes, put the fish, fish sauce, curry paste, lime leaf, cilantro, egg, sugar, and salt into the bowl of a food processor. Process until smooth. Scrape into a bowl and stir in the green beans. Set aside.

2 To make the dipping sauce, put the sugar, water, and rice vinegar into a small saucepan and heat gently until the sugar has dissolved. Bring to a boil and simmer for 2 minutes. Remove from the heat and stir in the chilies and fish sauce and leave to cool.

3 Heat a frying pan with enough oil to generously cover the bottom. Divide the fish mixture into 16 little balls. Flatten the balls into little patties and fry in the hot oil for 1–2 minutes each side until golden. Drain on paper towels. Serve hot with the dipping sauce.

COOK'S TIP

It isn't necessary to use the most expensive cut of white fish in this recipe as the other flavors are very strong. Use whatever is cheapest.

Maryland Crab Cakes with Basil & Tomato Dressing

Serves 4

INGREDIENTS

8 oz. potatoes, cut into chunks	2 tbsp. all-purpose flour	DRESSING
2 cups cooked white crab meat,	1 egg, lightly beaten	5 tbsp. olive oil
. thawed if frozen	1 cup fresh white breadcrumbs	1 tbsp. lemon juice
6 scallions, finely chopped	vegetable oil, for shallow frying	1 large ripe tomato, peeled,
1 small red chili, deseeded and	salt and pepper	deseeded and diced
finely chopped	lemon slices and dill, to serve	3 tbsp. chopped fresh basil
3 tbsp. mayonnaise		salt and pepper

1 Cook the potatoes in boiling salted water for 15–20 minutes until tender. Drain well and mash.

2 In a large bowl, mix together the crab meat, scallions, chili, and mayonnaise. Add the mashed potato, seasoning and mix together well. Shape the mixture into 8 cakes.

3 Put the flour, egg, and breadcrumbs into separate bowls. Dip the cakes first into the flour, then the egg and finally the breadcrumbs to coat. Refrigerate for 30 minutes.

4 In a large frying pan, heat enough vegetable oil to generously cover the bottom of the pan. Add the cakes, in batches if necessary, and cook for 3–4 minutes on each side until golden and crisp. Drain the cakes on paper towels and keep warm while you cook the remaining cakes.

5 Meanwhile, for the dressing, put the oil, lemon juice, and tomato in a small saucepan and heat gently for 2–3 minutes. Remove from the heat and stir in the basil and seasoning.

6 Divide the fish cakes between 4 serving plates. Spoon over the dressing. Serve immediately.

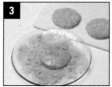

Lime & Basil Cured Salmon

Serves 6

INGREDIENTS

2 lb. very fresh salmon fillet, from the head end, skinned	DRESSING	TO GARNISH
¼ cup sugar	¾ cup rice vinegar	lime wedges
¼ cup sea salt	5 tbsp. sugar	basil leaves
5 tbsp. chopped fresh basil	finely grated rind of 1 lime	
finely grated rind of 2 limes	½ tsp. English mustard	
1 tsp. white peppercorns, lightly crushed	3 tbsp. chopped fresh basil	
	1 tbsp. Japanese pickled ginger, finely shredded	
	5½ oz. mixed salad leaves, to serve	

1 Remove any small bones that remain in the salmon fillet. Wash and dry the fish. Place the salmon in a large nonmetallic dish and sprinkle evenly with the sugar, sea salt, basil, lime rind, and peppercorns. Cover and chill for 24–48 hours, turning the fish occasionally.

2 For the dressing, put the rice vinegar and sugar in a small saucepan and stir gently over a low heat until the sugar has dissolved. Then, bring to a boil and simmer for 5–6 minutes until the liquid is reduced by about one third. Remove the saucepan from the heat and stir in the lime rind and mustard. Put the saucepan to one side.

3 Remove the salmon fillet from the marinade, wiping off any excess with paper towels. Slice the fillet very thinly.

4 To serve, stir the chopped basil and ginger into the dressing. Toss the salad leaves with a little of the dressing and arrange on 6 serving plates. Divide the salmon slices between the plates and drizzle a little dressing over. Garnish with lime wedges and basil leaves.

Hot-Smoked Salmon Scramble

Serves 4

INGREDIENTS

¼ cup butter
8 eggs, lightly beaten
4 tbsp. heavy cream
8 oz. skinless, boneless hot-
smoked salmon, flaked

2 tbsp. chopped fresh mixed
herbs such as chives, basil,
and parsley
4 English muffins, split
extra butter, for spreading

salt and pepper
chopped fresh chives, to garnish
lemon wedges, to serve

1 Melt the butter in a large frying pan and when it begins to foam, add the eggs. Leave for a moment to start to set and slowly stir and move the set eggs away from the bottom of the pan to allow uncooked egg to take its place. Leave again for a moment and repeat.

2 Before all the egg has set, stir in the heavy cream, flaked salmon, and chopped herbs. Stir to incorporate. Do not overcook the eggs.

3 Meanwhile, toast the split muffins on both sides. Spread with more butter if desired. Place 2 muffin halves on each of four plates.

4 When the eggs are cooked, divide between the muffins. Sprinkle over a few chopped chives, season and serve while still warm with a lemon wedge.

VARIATION

If you have difficulty finding hot-smoked salmon, you could substitute conventional smoked salmon, chopped.

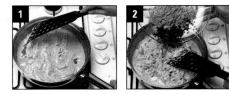

Griddle Smoked Salmon

Serves 4

INGREDIENTS

12 oz. sliced smoked salmon	2 tsp. sherry vinegar
1 tsp. Dijon mustard	4 tbsp. olive oil
1 garlic clove, crushed	4 oz. mixed salad leaves
2 tsp. chopped fresh dill	salt and pepper

1 Take the slices of smoked salmon and fold them, making two folds accordion style, so that they form little parcels.

2 Whisk the mustard, garlic, dill, vinegar, and seasoning together. Gradually whisk in the olive oil to form a light emulsion.

3 Heat a ridged griddle until smoking. Cook the salmon bundles on one side only for 2–3 minutes until heated through and marked from the pan.

4 Meanwhile, dress the salad leaves with some of the vinaigrette and divide between four serving plates. Top with the salmon, cooked side up. Drizzle with the remaining dressing.

COOK'S TIP

Smoked salmon is very expensive. This recipe would also work well with smoked trout.

Salmon Tartare

Serves 6

INGREDIENTS

2 lb. very fresh salmon
   fillet, skinned
3 tbsp. lemon juice
3 tbsp. lime juice
2 tsp. sugar
1 tsp. Dijon mustard
1 tbsp. chopped fresh dill

1 tbsp. chopped fresh basil
2 tbsp. olive oil
1¾ oz. arugula
handful basil leaves
1¾ oz. mixed salad leaves
salt and pepper

TO GARNISH
dill sprigs
basil leaves

1 Cut the salmon into very tiny dice and season. Put into a large bowl.

2 Mix together the lemon juice, lime juice, sugar, mustard, dill, basil, and olive oil. Pour over the salmon and mix well. Set aside for 15–20 minutes until the fish becomes opaque.

3 Meanwhile, mix together the arugula, basil leaves, and salad leaves. Divide the leaves between six serving plates.

4 To serve the salmon, fill a small ramekin with the mixture and turn out on to the center of the salad leaves. Garnish with dill sprigs and basil leaves.

VARIATION

Haddock also responds very well to this treatment. Use half the quantity of salmon and an equal weight of haddock.

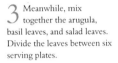

Gravadlax

Serves 6

INGREDIENTS

2 x 1 lb. salmon fillets, with
skin on
6 tbsp. roughly chopped fresh dill
¼ cup sea salt
¼ cup sugar

1 tbsp. white peppercorns,
roughly crushed
12 slices brown bread, buttered,
to serve

GARNISH
lemon slices
dill sprigs

1 Wash the salmon fillets and dry with paper towels. Place one fillet, skin side down, in a nonmetallic dish.

2 Mix together the dill, sea salt, sugar, and peppercorns. Spread this mixture over the first fillet of fish and place the second fillet, skin side up, on top. Put a plate, the same size as the fish, on top and put a weight on the plate (such as 3 or 4 cans of tomatoes).

3 Refrigerate for 2 days, turning the fish about every 12 hours and basting with any juices which have come out of the fish.

4 Remove the salmon from the brine and slice thinly, without slicing the skin, as you would smoked salmon. Cut the brown bread into triangles and serve with the salmon. Garnish with lemon wedges and sprigs of fresh dill.

COOK'S TIP

You can brush the marinade off the salmon before slicing, but the line of green along the edge of the salmon is quite attractive and, of course, full of flavor.

Thai Crab Omelet

Serves 4

INGREDIENTS

8 oz. white crab meat, fresh or thawed if frozen	2 garlic cloves, crushed	2 tsp. Thai fish sauce
3 scallions, finely chopped	1 tsp. freshly grated ginger root	3 eggs
1 tbsp. chopped cilantro	1 red chili, deseeded and finely chopped	4 tbsp. coconut cream
1 tbsp. chopped fresh chives	2 tbsp. lime juice	1 tsp. salt
pinch cayenne pepper	2 lime leaves, shredded	1 tbsp. vegetable oil
1 tbsp. vegetable oil	2 tsp. sugar	scallion slivers, to garnish

1 Put the crab meat into a bowl and check for any small pieces of shell. Add the scallions, cilantro, chives, and cayenne and set aside.

2 Heat the vegetable oil and add the garlic, ginger, and chili and stir-fry for 30 seconds. Add the lime juice, lime leaves, sugar and fish sauce. Simmer for 3–4 minutes until reduced. Remove from the heat and allow to cool. Add to the crab mixture and set aside.

3 Lightly beat the eggs with the coconut cream and salt. In a frying pan, heat the vegetable oil over a medium heat. Add the egg mixture and as it sets on the bottom, carefully pull the edges in toward the center, allowing unset egg to run underneath.

4 When the egg is nearly set, spoon the crab mixture down the center. Cook an additional 1–2 minutes to finish cooking the egg, then turn the omelet out of the pan on to a serving dish. Allow to cool then refrigerate for 2–3 hours or overnight. Cut into 4 pieces and garnish with scallion.

COOK'S TIP

You can also serve this omelet warm. After adding the crab, cook for 3–4 minutes to allow the mixture to heat through then serve immediately.

Soups & Stews

Using seafood in soups and stews makes wonderful sense. It doesn't require much cooking, making it ideal as a basis for a midweek supper, and it combines well with an enormous variety of flavors.

It seems that only in the English-speaking world is fish undervalued. Other parts of the world use fish as a staple part of their diet and this chapter includes many dishes from a variety of places.

Don't worry though, most of the more unusual ingredients are readily available nowadays from larger supermarkets or from specialty shops. Soups like Thai Fish Soup, Malaysian Seafood Laksa, and Chinese Crab & Sweetcorn Soup illustrate the diversity of the recipes. Some of the soups are very subtly flavored and ideal as a first course at a dinner party, such as the Creamy Scallop Soup.

Others are much more substantial and could easily be served as a main course, like the Cullen Skink. There are lots of stews and curries to choose from as well, from Red Shrimp Curry to Goan Fish Curry and from Cotriade to Spanish Fish Stew.

Thai Fish Soup

Serves 4

INGREDIENTS

2 cups light chicken stock

2 lime leaves, chopped

2 inch piece lemon grass, chopped

3 tbsp. lemon juice

3 tbsp. Thai fish sauce

2 small, hot green chilies, deseeded and finely chopped

½ tsp. sugar

8 small shiitake mushrooms or 8 straw mushrooms, halved

1 lb. raw shrimp, peeled if necessary and de-veined

scallions, to garnish

TOM YAM SAUCE

4 tbsp. vegetable oil

5 garlic cloves, finely chopped

1 large shallot, finely chopped

2 large hot dried red chilies, roughly chopped

1 tbsp. dried shrimp (optional)

1 tbsp. Thai fish sauce

2 tsp. sugar

1 First make the tom yam sauce. Heat the oil in a small frying pan and add the garlic. Cook for a few seconds until the garlic just browns. Remove with a slotted spoon and set aside. Add the shallot to the same oil and fry until browned and crisp. Remove with a slotted spoon and set aside. Add the chilies and fry until they darken. Remove from the oil and drain on paper towels. Remove from heat, reserving the oil.

2 In a small food processor or spice grinder, grind the dried shrimp, if using, then add the reserved chilies, garlic, and shallots. Grind together to a smooth paste. Return the pan with the original oil to a low heat, add the paste and warm. Add the fish sauce and sugar and mix. Remove from the heat.

3 In a large saucepan, heat together the stock and 2 tablespoons of the tom yam sauce. Add the lime leaves, lemon grass, lemon juice, fish sauce, chilies, and sugar. Simmer for 2 minutes.

4 Add the mushrooms and shrimp and cook an additional 2–3 minutes until the shrimp are cooked. Ladle into warm bowls and serve immediately, garnished with scallions.

Cullen Skink

Serves 4

INGREDIENTS

8 oz. smoked haddock fillet	12 oz. cod, boned, skinned	TO GARNISH
2 tbsp. butter	and cubed	lemon slices
1 onion, finely chopped	⅔ cup heavy cream	parsley sprigs
2½ cups milk	2 tbsp. chopped fresh parsley	
12 oz. potatoes, cut into dice	lemon juice, to taste	
	salt and pepper	

1 Put the haddock fillet in a large frying pan and cover with boiling water. Leave for 10 minutes. Drain, reserving 1 cup of the soaking water. Flake the fish, taking care to remove all of the bones.

2 Heat the butter in a large saucepan and add the onion. Cook gently for 10 minutes until softened. Add the milk and bring to a gentle simmer before adding the potato. Cook for 10 minutes.

3 Add the reserved haddock flakes and cod. Simmer for another 10 minutes until the cod is tender.

4 Remove about one third of the fish and potatoes, put in a food processor and blend until smooth. Alternatively, push through a sieve into a bowl. Return to the soup with the cream, parsley, and seasoning. Taste and add a little lemon juice, if desired. Add a little of the reserved soaking water if the soup seems too thick. Reheat gently and serve immediately.

COOK'S TIP

Look for Finnan haddock, if you can find it. Do not use yellow-dyed haddock fillet, which is often actually whiting and not haddock at all.

New England Clam Chowder

Serves 4

INGREDIENTS

2 lb. live clams

4 slices bacon, chopped

2 tbsp. butter

1 onion, chopped

1 tbsp. chopped fresh thyme

1 large potato, diced

1 bay leaf

1¼ cups milk

1⅔ cup heavy cream

1 tbsp. chopped fresh parsley

salt and pepper

reserve 8 clams in their shells,
to garnish (see Cook's Tip)

1 Scrub the clams and put into a large saucepan with a splash of water. Cook over a high heat for 3–4 minutes until all the clams have opened. Discard any that remain closed. Strain the clams, reserving the cooking liquid. Set aside until cool enough to handle.

2 Remove the clams from their shells, roughly chop if large, and set aside.

3 In a clean saucepan, fry the bacon until browned and crisp. Drain on paper towels. Add the butter to the same pan and when it has melted, add the onion. Cook for 4–5 minutes until softened but not colored. Add the thyme and cook briefly before adding the diced potato, reserved clam cooking liquid, milk and bay leaf. Bring to a boil and simmer for 10 minutes until the potato is tender but not falling apart.

4 Transfer to a food processor and blend until smooth or push through a sieve into a bowl.

5 Add the reserved clams, bacon and the cream. Simmer an additional 2–3 minutes until heated through. Season to taste. Stir in the chopped parsley and serve.

COOK'S TIP

For a smart presentation, reserve 8 clams in their shells. Sit 2 on top of each bowl of soup to serve.

Malaysian Seafood Laksa

Serves 4

INGREDIENTS

8 raw jumbo shrimp	LAKSA SPICE PASTE	TO GARNISH
1 small squid, about 4 oz. cleaned weight	3 large dried red chilies	½ cucumber, cut into matchsticks
4 tbsp. vegetable oil	1 oz. dried shrimp (optional)	1 tbsp. chopped cilantro
3½ cups light chicken stock	2 stalks lemon grass, chopped	1 tbsp. chopped fresh mint
8 oz. medium egg noodles	½ cup macadamia nuts	4 scallions, thinly sliced
4 oz. beansprouts	2 garlic cloves, chopped	1 red chili, sliced into rings
14 oz. can coconut milk	2 tsp. chopped fresh ginger	1 lime, quartered
2 tsp. muscovado sugar	1 tsp. turmeric	
1 tsp. salt	1 small onion, chopped	
	1 tsp. ground cilantro	
	3 tbsp. water	

1 For the laksa spice paste, soak the dried chilies in boiling water for 10 minutes. Drain (remove the seeds if you prefer) and blend in a food processor with the remaining paste ingredients.

2 Peel the shrimp if necessary and de-vein. Split the squid down one side and open out flat.

Lightly score the underside of the flesh using a sharp knife. Cut into 1 in. squares; set aside.

3 Heat the vegetable oil in a large saucepan and fry the spice paste gently for 5–6 minutes until it smells very fragrant. Add the stock, bring to a boil, cover and simmer gently for 20 minutes.

4 Cook the egg noodles according to the packet instructions, drain well and set aside. Blanch the beansprouts for 1 minute and refresh under cold water. Drain well and set aside.

5 Add the coconut milk to the stock and simmer for 3 minutes. Add the shrimp, squid, sugar and salt and simmer for just 4 minutes until the seafood is tender.

6 Divide the noodles and beansprouts between 4 warmed soup bowls. Spoon on the hot soup and sprinkle with the garnish.

Chinese Crab & Corn Soup

Serves 4

INGREDIENTS

1 tbsp. vegetable oil
1 small onion, finely chopped
1 garlic clove, finely chopped
1 tsp. grated fresh ginger

1 small red chili, deseeded and
  finely chopped
2 tbsp. dry sherry or Chinese
  rice wine
8 oz. fresh white crab meat
11 oz. can corn, drained

2½ cups light chicken stock
1 tbsp. light soy sauce
2 tbsp. chopped cilantro
2 eggs, beaten
salt and pepper

1 Heat the oil in a large saucepan and add the onion. Cook gently for 5 minutes until softened. Add the garlic, ginger, and chili and cook for an additional minute.

2 Add the sherry or rice wine and bubble until reduced by half. Add the crab meat, corn, chicken stock, and soy sauce. Bring to a boil and simmer gently for 5 minutes. Stir in the cilantro. Season to taste.

3 Remove from the heat and pour in the eggs. Wait for a few seconds and then stir well, to break the eggs into ribbons. Serve immediately, garnished with a chili cut into a tassel.

COOK'S TIP

For convenience, you could use canned crab meat. Make sure it is well drained before adding it to the soup.

Creamy Scallop Soup

Serves 4

INGREDIENTS

¼ cup butter	12 oz. prepared scallops,	¾ cup heavy cream
1 onion, finely chopped	including corals if available	salt and pepper
1 lb. potatoes, diced	1¼ cups milk	1 tbsp. chopped fresh parsley,
2½ cups hot fish stock	2 egg yolks	to garnish

1 Melt the butter in a large saucepan over a gentle heat. Add the onions and cook very gently for 10 minutes until the onions are softened but not colored. Add the potatoes and seasoning, cover and cook for an additional 10 minutes over a very low heat.

2 Pour on the hot fish stock, bring to a boil and simmer for an additional 10–15 minutes until the potatoes are tender.

3 Meanwhile, prepare the scallops. If the corals are available, roughly chop and set aside. Roughly chop the white meat and put in a second saucepan with the milk. Bring to a gentle simmer and cook for 6–8 minutes until the scallops are just tender.

4 When the potatoes are cooked, transfer them and their cooking liquid to a food processor or blender and blend to a purée. Alternatively, press through a nylon sieve. Return the mixture to a clean saucepan with the scallops and their milk and the pieces of coral, if using.

5 Whisk together the egg yolks and cream and add to the soup, off the heat. Return the soup to a very gentle heat and, stirring constantly, reheat the soup until it thickens slightly. Do not boil or the soup will curdle. Serve hot, sprinkled with fresh parsley.

COOK'S TIP

The soup can be made in advance up to the point where the cream and eggs are added. This should only be done just before serving.

Curried Mussel Soup

Serves 4

INGREDIENTS

½ tsp. coriander seeds	1 onion, finely chopped	4 tbsp. heavy cream
½ tsp. cumin seeds	1 garlic clove, finely chopped	2 tbsp. butter, softened
2 lb. live mussels	1 tsp. freshly grated ginger	2 tbsp. flour
scant ½ cup	1 tsp. turmeric	2 tbsp. chopped cilantro,
white wine	pinch cayenne pepper	to garnish
¼ cup butter	2½ cups fish stock	salt and pepper

1 Fry the coriander and cumin seeds in a dry frying pan until they begin to smell aromatic and start to pop. Grind to a powder with a pestle and mortar. Set aside.

2 Clean the mussels by scrubbing or scraping the shells and pulling out any beards that are attached to them. Discard any with broken shells or any that do not close when tapped. Put the mussels into a large pan with the wine and cook, covered, over a high heat for 3–4 minutes, shaking the pan occasionally, until all the mussels have opened. Discard any mussels that remain closed. Drain, reserving the cooking liquid, and set aside until the mussels are cool enough to handle. Remove about two-thirds of the mussels from their shells and set them all aside. Strain the mussel cooking liquid through a fine sieve.

3 Heat half the butter in a large saucepan and add the onion. Fry gently for 4–5 minutes until softened, but not colored. Add the garlic and ginger and cook for an additional minute before adding the roasted and ground spices, the turmeric, and cayenne. Fry for 1 minute before adding the fish stock, reserved mussel cooking liquid, and cream. Simmer for 10 minutes.

4 Cream together the butter and flour to a thick paste. Add the paste to the simmering soup and stir until dissolved and the soup has thickened slightly. Add the mussels and warm for 2 minutes. Garnish with chopped cilantro.

Clam & Sorrel Soup

Serves 4

INGREDIENTS

2 lb. live clams, scrubbed	2 shallots, finely diced	pepper, to taste
1 onion, finely chopped	1 stalk celery, finely diced	crusty bread, to serve
⅔ cup dry white wine	2 bay leaves	dill, to garnish
¼ cup butter	⅔ cup heavy cream	
1 small carrot, finely diced	1 cup loosely packed shredded sorrel	

1 Put the clams into a large saucepan with the onion and wine. Cover and cook over a high heat for 3–4 minutes until the clams have opened. Strain, reserving the cooking liquid, but discarding the onion. Set aside the clams until they are cool enough to handle.

2 In a clean saucepan, melt the butter over a low heat. Add the carrot, shallots, and celery and cook very gently for 10 minutes until softened but not colored. Add the reserved cooking liquid and bay leaves and simmer for an additional 10 minutes.

3 Meanwhile, roughly chop the clams, if large. Add to the soup with the cream and sorrel. Simmer an additional 2–3 minutes until the sorrel has collapsed. Season with pepper and serve immediately with plenty of crusty bread.

COOK'S TIP

Sorrel is an herb with a slightly sour, lemony flavor that goes very well with fish. It is increasingly easy to find in larger supermarkets, but is also incredibly easy to grow as a plant.

Basque Tuna Stew

Serves 4

INGREDIENTS

5 tbsp. olive oil
1 large onion, chopped
2 garlic cloves, chopped
7 oz. can chopped tomatoes

1 lb. 9 oz. potatoes, cut into
2 inch chunks
3 green bell peppers, deseeded
and roughly chopped

1¼ cups cold water
2 lb. fresh tuna, cut into chunks
4 slices crusty white bread
salt and pepper

1 Heat 2 tablespoons of the oil in a saucepan and add the onion. Cook for 8–10 minutes until soft and brown. Add the garlic and cook an additional minute. Add the tomatoes, cover and simmer for 30 minutes until thickened.

2 Meanwhile, in a clean saucepan, mix together the potatoes and peppers. Add the water (which should just cover the vegetables). Bring to a boil and simmer for 15 minutes until the potatoes are almost tender.

3 Add the tuna and the tomato mixture to the potatoes and peppers and season. Cover and simmer for 6–8 minutes until tuna is tender.

4 Meanwhile, heat the remaining oil in a large frying pan over a medium heat and add the bread slices. Fry on both sides until golden. Drain on paper towels. Serve with the stew.

VARIATION

Substitute any very firm-fleshed fish, such as shark or swordfish for the tuna used in this recipe.

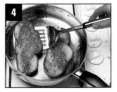

Goan Fish Curry

Serves 4

INGREDIENTS

1½ lb. monkfish fillet, cut into chunks
1 tbsp. cider vinegar
1 tsp. salt
1 tsp. ground turmeric
3 tbsp. vegetable oil

2 garlic cloves, crushed
1 small onion, finely chopped
2 tsp. ground coriander
1 tsp. cayenne pepper
2 tsp. paprika

2 tbsp. tamarind pulp plus 2 tbsp. boiling water (see method)
3 oz. creamed coconut, cut into pieces
1¼ cups warm water
plain boiled rice, to serve

1 Put the fish on a plate and drizzle over the vinegar. Mix together half the salt and half the turmeric and sprinkle evenly over the fish. Cover and set aside for 20 minutes.

2 Heat the oil in a frying pan and add the garlic. Brown slightly then add the onion and fry for 3–4 minutes until soft, but not browned. Add the ground coriander and stir for 1 minute.

3 Mix the remaining turmeric, cayenne, and paprika with about 2 tablespoons water to make a paste. Add this to the pan and cook over a low heat for 1–2 minutes.

4 Mix the tamarind pulp with the 2 tablespoons boiling water and stir well. When the water appears thick and the pulp has come away from the seeds, pass this mixture through a sieve, rubbing the pulp well.

Discard the seeds once you have finished.

5 Add the coconut, warm water, and tamarind paste to the pan and stir until the coconut has dissolved. Add the pieces of fish and any juices on the plate and simmer gently for 4–5 minutes until the sauce has thickened and the fish is just tender. Serve immediately on a bed of plain boiled rice.

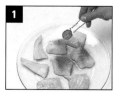

Thai Green Fish Curry

Serves 4

INGREDIENTS

2 tbsp. vegetable oil
1 garlic clove, chopped
1 small eggplant, diced
½ cup coconut cream
2 tbsp. Thai fish sauce
1 tsp. sugar
8 oz. firm white fish, cut into pieces, such as cod, haddock, or halibut
½ cup fish stock
2 lime leaves, finely shredded

about 15 leaves Thai basil, if available, or ordinary basil
plain boiled rice or noodles, to serve

GREEN CURRY PASTE
5 fresh green chilies, deseeded and chopped
2 tsp. chopped lemon grass
1 large shallot, chopped
2 garlic cloves, chopped

1 tsp. freshly grated ginger or galangal, if available
2 coriander roots, chopped
½ tsp. ground coriander
¼ tsp. ground cumin
1 kaffir lime leaf, finely chopped
1 tsp. shrimp paste (optional)
½ tsp. salt

1 Make the curry paste. Put all the ingredients into a blender or spice grinder and blend to a smooth paste, adding a little water if necessary. Alternatively, pound the ingredients, using a mortar and pestle, until smooth. Set aside.

2 In a frying pan or wok, heat the oil until almost smoking and add the garlic.

Fry until golden. Add the curry paste and stir-fry a few seconds before adding the eggplant. Stir-fry for about 4–5 minutes until softened.

3 Add the coconut cream. Bring to a boil and stir until the cream thickens and curdles slightly. Add the fish sauce and sugar to the frying pan and then stir in to combine thoroughly.

4 Add the fish pieces and stock. Simmer for 3–4 minutes, stirring occasionally, until the fish is just tender. Add the lime leaves and basil, and then cook for an additional minute. Remove from the frying pan and serve hot with plain boiled rice or noodles.

Mackerel Escabeche

Serves 4

INGREDIENTS

⅔ cup olive oil
4 mackerel, filleted
2 tbsp. seasoned flour,
    for dusting
4 tbsp. red wine vinegar
1 onion, finely sliced

1 strip orange rind, removed
    with a potato peeler
1 sprig fresh thyme
1 sprig fresh rosemary
1 fresh bay leaf

4 garlic cloves, crushed
2 fresh red chilies, bruised
1 tsp. salt
3 tbsp. chopped fresh
    flat-leaf parsley
crusty bread, to serve

1 Heat half the oil in a frying pan and dust the mackerel fillets with the seasoned flour.

2 Add the fish to the frying pan and then cook for about 30 seconds each side until not quite cooked through.

3 Transfer the mackerel to a shallow dish, large enough to hold the fillets in one layer.

4 Add the the vinegar, onion, orange rind, thyme, rosemary, garlic, chilies, and salt to the pan. Simmer for 10 minutes.

5 Add the remaining olive oil and the chopped parsley. Pour the mixture over the fish and leave until cold. Serve with plenty of fresh crusty bread.

VARIATION

Substitute 12 whole sardines, cleaned, with heads removed. Cook in the same way. Tuna steaks are also very delicious served escabeche.

Lemon Sole in a Sweet & Sour Sauce

Serves 4

INGREDIENTS

2 large lemon sole, filleted
flour, to dredge
olive oil, to deep-fry plus
    2 tbsp. olive oil
2 onions, sliced thinly

1 cup hazelnuts, chopped
½ cup pine nuts
¼ cup raisins
8 oz. ripe tomatoes, skinned,
    and chopped

2 tbsp. red wine vinegar
½ cup water
3 tbsp. chopped fresh parsley
salt and pepper
boiled new potatoes, to serve

1 Wash and dry the fish fillets. Dredge lightly with flour. In a large frying pan, heat about 1 inch of olive oil—enough to just cover the fish—over a medium-high heat. Add the fish fillets, 2 at a time, and completely submerge in the oil. Cook for 5–6 minutes then drain on paper towels. Set aside. Cook the rest of the fish in the same way.

2 Heat the remaining 2 tablespoons of olive oil in a large saucepan. Add the onions and cook for 7–8 minutes until soft and starting to brown. Add the hazelnuts, pine nuts, and raisins and fry for an additional 1–2 minutes until the nuts are golden. Add the tomatoes and cook for 5 minutes until softened.

3 Add the vinegar and simmer for 5 minutes. Add the water, parsley and seasoning and stir well. Simmer an additional 5 minutes.

4 Lower the fried fish into the sauce and simmer gently for 10 minutes. Serve with boiled new potatoes.

COOK'S TIP

In the Middle East, many different types of fish are treated this way, but a particular favorite is red mullet. Small fish can be left whole (after cleaning and scaling).

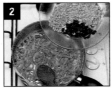

Haddock Baked in Yogurt

Serves 4

INGREDIENTS

2 large onions, thinly sliced
2 lb. haddock fillet, from the head end
scant 2 cups plain yogurt
2 tbsp. lemon juice

1 tsp. sugar
2 tsp. ground cumin
2 tsp. ground coriander
pinch garam masala
pinch cayenne pepper, to taste

1 tsp. freshly grated ginger
3 tbsp. vegetable oil
¼ cup cold unsalted butter, cut into pieces
salt and pepper

1 Line a large baking dish with the onion slices. Cut the haddock into strips widthwise and then lay them in a single layer over the onions.

2 In a bowl, mix together the yogurt, lemon juice, sugar, cumin, coriander, garam masala, cayenne, ginger, oil and seasoning. Pour this sauce over the fish, making sure it goes under the fish as well. Cover tightly.

3 Bake in a preheated oven at 375° F for 30 minutes or until the fish is just tender.

4 Carefully pour the sauce off the fish into a pan. Bring to a boil and simmer to reduce to about 1½ cups. Remove from the heat.

5 Add the cubes of butter to the sauce and whisk until melted and incorporated. Pour the sauce back over the fish and serve.

COOK'S TIP

When you pour the sauce off the fish it will look thin and separated, but reducing and stirring in the butter will help to thicken it.

Cod Italienne

Serves 4

INGREDIENTS

2 tbsp. olive oil
1 onion, finely chopped
2 garlic clove, finely chopped
2 tsp. freshly chopped thyme
²/₃ cup red wine
2 x 14 oz. cans chopped
    tomatoes
pinch sugar

¼ cup pitted black olives,
    roughly chopped
¼ cup pitted green olives,
    roughly chopped
2 tbsp. capers, drained, rinsed,
    and roughly chopped
2 tbsp. chopped fresh basil

4 cod steaks, each weighing
    about 6 oz.
5½ oz. ball buffalo mozzarella,
    drained and sliced
salt and pepper
buttered noodles, to serve

1 Heat the olive oil in a large saucepan. Add the onion and fry gently for 5 minutes until softened but not colored. Add the garlic and thyme and cook an additional minute.

2 Add the red wine and increase the heat. Simmer until reduced and syrupy. Add the tomatoes and sugar and bring to a boil. Cover and simmer for 30 minutes. Uncover and simmer an additional 20 minutes until thick. Stir in the olives, capers, and basil. Season to taste.

3 Arrange the cod steaks in a shallow ovenproof dish (a lasagne dish is perfect) and spoon the tomato sauce over the top. Bake in a preheated oven at 375° F for 20–25 minutes, until the fish is just tender.

4 Remove from the oven and arrange the mozzarella slices on top of the fish steaks.

5 Return to the oven for an additional 5–10 minutes until the cheese has melted. Serve immediately with buttered noodles.

VARIATION

Other white fish steaks would work equally well and, if you want to experiment, try turbot.

Cod Curry

Serves 4

INGREDIENTS

1 tbsp. vegetable oil
1 small onion, chopped
2 garlic cloves, chopped
1 in. piece fresh ginger,
  roughly chopped
2 large ripe tomatoes, skinned
  and roughly chopped

²/₃ cup fish stock
1 tbsp. medium curry paste
1 tsp. ground coriander
14 oz. can chickpeas, drained
  and rinsed
1½ lb. cod fillet, cut into
  large chunks

4 tbsp. chopped cilantro
4 tbsp. plain yogurt
salt and pepper
steamed basmati rice, to serve

1 Heat the oil in a large saucepan and add the onion, garlic and ginger. Fry for 4–5 minutes until softened. Remove from the heat. Put the onion mixture into a food processor or blender with the tomatoes and fish stock and blend until smooth.

2 Return to the saucepan with the curry paste, ground coriander and chickpeas. Mix together well then simmer gently for 15 minutes until thickened.

3 Add the pieces of fish and return to a simmer. Cook for 5 minutes until the fish is just tender. Remove from the heat and leave to stand for 2–3 minutes.

4 Stir in the cilantro and yogurt. Season and serve with steamed basmati rice.

VARIATION

Instead of cod, make this curry using raw shrimp and then omit the chickpeas.

Home-Salted Cod with Chickpeas

Serves 6

INGREDIENTS

3 lb. 5oz. fresh boneless cod fillet, from the head end, skin on

8 oz. dried chickpeas, soaked for 8 hours or overnight

1 fresh red chili

4 garlic cloves

2 bay leaves

1 tbsp. olive oil

1¼ cups chicken stock

pepper, to taste

extra-virgin olive oil, to drizzle

GREMOLATA

3 tbsp. chopped fresh parsley

2 garlic cloves, finely chopped

finely grated rind of 1 lemon

1 Sprinkle the salt over both sides of the cod fillet. Place in a shallow dish, cover and refrigerate for 48 hours. When ready to cook, remove cod from the refrigerator and rinse under cold water. Leave to soak in cold water for 2 hours.

2 Drain the chickpeas, rinse them thoroughly, and drain again. Put into a large saucepan. Add double their volume of water and bring slowly to a boil. Skim the surface. Split the chili lengthwise and add to the chickpeas with the whole garlic cloves and bay leaves. Cover and simmer for 1½–2 hours until very tender, skimming occasionally if necessary.

3 Drain the cod and pat dry. Brush with the olive oil and season well with black pepper (but no salt). Cook under a preheated broiler or on a hot, ridged griddle for 3–4 minutes on each side until tender. Meanwhile, add the chicken stock to the chickpeas and bring back to a boil. Keep warm.

4 For the gremolata, mix together the parsley, garlic, and finely grated lemon rind.

5 To serve, ladle the chickpeas and their cooking liquid into 6 warmed soup bowls. Top with the broiled cod and sprinkle over the gremolata. Drizzle generously with olive oil and serve.

Cotriade

Serves 6

INGREDIENTS

large pinch saffron
2½ cups hot fish stock
1 tbsp. olive oil
2 tbsp. butter
1 onion, sliced
2 garlic cloves, chopped
1 leek, sliced

1 small fennel bulb, finely sliced
1 lb. potatoes, cut into chunks
⅔ cup dry white wine
1 tbsp. fresh thyme leaves
2 bay leaves
4 ripe tomatoes, skinned
    and chopped

2 lb. mixed fish such as haddock,
    hake, mackerel, red or gray
    mullet, roughly chopped
2 tbsp. chopped fresh parsley
salt and pepper
crusty bread, to serve

1 Using a mortar and pestle, crush the saffron and add to the fish stock. Stir and leave to infuse for at least 10 minutes.

2 In a large saucepan, heat the oil and butter together. Add the onion and cook gently for 4–5 minutes until softened. Add the garlic, leek, fennel and potatoes. Cover the pan and then cook for an additional 10–15 minutes until the vegetables are softened.

3 Add the wine and simmer rapidly for 3–4 minutes until reduced by half. Add the thyme, bay leaves, and tomatoes and stir well. Add the saffron-infused fish stock. Bring to a boil, cover and simmer gently for 15 minutes until the vegetables are tender.

4 Add the fish, return to a boil and simmer for an additional 3–4 minutes until all the fish is tender. Add the parsley and season to taste.

Using a slotted spoon, remove the fish and vegetables to a warmed serving dish. Serve the soup with plenty of crusty bread.

VARIATION

Once the fish and vegetables have been cooked, you could process the soup and pass it through a sieve to give a smooth fish soup.

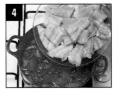

Squid Stew

Serves 4

INGREDIENTS

1 lb. 10 oz. squid	1 tsp. fresh thyme leaves	1 tbsp. chopped fresh parsley
3 tbsp. olive oil	14 oz. can chopped tomatoes	salt and pepper
1 onion, chopped	²⁄₃ cup red wine	
3 garlic cloves, finely chopped	1¼ cups water	

1 To prepare whole squid, hold the body firmly and grasp the tentacles just inside the body. Pull firmly to remove the innards. Find the transparent "backbone" and remove. Grasp the wings on the outside of the body and pull to remove the outer skin. Trim the tentacles just below the beak and reserve. Wash the body and tentacles under running water. Slice the body into rings. Drain well on paper towels.

2 Heat the oil in a large, flameproof casserole. Add the prepared squid and cook over a medium heat, stirring occasionally, until lightly browned.

3 Reduce the heat and add the onion, garlic and thyme. Cook an additional 5 minutes until softened.

4 Stir in the tomatoes, red wine and water. Bring to a boil and cook to a preheated oven at 275° F for 2 hours. Stir in the parsley and season to taste.

VARIATION

This stew can be used as the basis for a more substantial fish stew. Before adding the parsley, add extra seafood such as scallops, pieces of fish fillet, jumbo shrimp, or even cooked lobster. Return the stew to a boil and cook an additional 2 minutes. Add the parsley and seasoning.

Spanish Fish Stew

Serves 6

INGREDIENTS

5 tbsp. olive oil

2 large onions, finely chopped

2 ripe tomatoes, skinned, deseeded and diced

2 slices white bread, crusts removed

4 almonds, toasted

3 garlic cloves, roughly chopped

12 oz. cooked lobster

7 oz. cleaned squid

7 oz. monkfish fillet

7 oz. cod fillet, skinned

1 tbsp. all-purpose flour

6 large jumbo shrimp

6 langoustines

18 live mussels, scrubbed, beards removed

8 large live clams, scrubbed

1 tbsp. chopped fresh parsley

½ cup brandy

salt and pepper

1 Heat 3 tablespoons of the oil in a frying pan, add the onions and cook gently for 10–15 minutes until lightly golden, adding a little water to prevent them sticking, if necessary. Add the tomatoes and cook until they have melted down and the oil has separated away from them.

2 Heat 1 tablespoon of the remaining oil and fry the slices of bread until crisp. Break into rough pieces and put into a mortar with the almonds and 2 garlic cloves. Pound together to make a fine paste. Alternatively, blend the mixture to a paste in a food processor.

3 To prepare the lobster, split it lengthwise. Remove and discard the intestinal vein which runs down the tail, the stomach sac and the spongy-looking gills. Crack the claws and remove the meat. Take out the flesh from the tail and chop into large chunks. Slice the squid into rings.

4 Season the monkfish, cod, and lobster and dust with a little flour. In a frying pan, heat a little oil and brown the fish separately: monkfish, cod, lobster; then squid, shrimp, langoustines. Arrange in a flameproof casserole as they brown.

5 Add the mussels, clams, remaining garlic and parsley to the browned fish. Place over a low heat, pour over the brandy and ignite. When the flames have died down, add the tomato mixture and just enough water to cover. Bring to a boil and simmer for 3–4 minutes until the mussels and clams have opened. Discard any that remain closed. Stir in the bread mixture and season to taste. Simmer for 5 minutes until all the fish is tender.

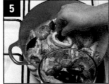

Moroccan Fish Tagine

Serves 4

INGREDIENTS

2 tbsp olive oil
1 large onion, finely chopped
large pinch saffron strands
½ tsp ground cinnamon
1 tsp ground coriander
½ tsp ground cumin

½ tsp ground turmeric
7 oz can chopped tomatoes
1¼ cups fish stock
4 small red mullet cleaned, boned and heads and tails removed

1¾ oz pitted green olives
1 tbsp chopped preserved lemon
3 tbsp fresh chopped cilantro
salt and pepper
couscous, to serve

1 Heat the olive oil in a large pan or flameproof casserole. Add the onion and cook gently for 10 minutes without coloring until softened. Add the saffron, cinnamon, ground coriander, cumin, and turmeric and cook for an additional 30 seconds, stirring.

2 Add the chopped tomatoes and fish stock and stir well. Bring to a boil, then cover and simmer for 15 minutes. Uncover the pan and simmer for an additional 20–35 minutes until thickened.

3 Cut each red mullet in half then add the pieces to the pan, pushing them into the sauce. Simmer gently for an additional 5–6 minutes until the fish is just cooked.

4 Carefully stir in the olives, preserved lemon and the chopped cilantro. Season to taste and serve with couscous.

COOK'S TIP

Preserved lemons are simple to make yourself. Take enough lemons to completely fill a preserving jar and quarter them lengthwise without cutting all the way through. Pack the lemons with ¼ cup sea salt per lemon, adding any remaining salt to the jar. Add the juice of a further lemon and top up with water to cover. Leave for at least 1 month before using.

Stewed Sardines

Serves 4

INGREDIENTS

¾ cup raisins

3 tbsp. Marsala

4 tbsp. olive oil

8 oz. baby onions, halved if large

2 garlic cloves, chopped

1 tbsp. chopped fresh sage

4 large tomatoes, skinned and chopped

⅔ cup fish or vegetable stock

2 tbsp. balsamic vinegar

1 lb. fresh sardines, cleaned

¼ cup pitted black olives

1 oz. pine nuts, toasted

2 tbsp. chopped fresh parsley

1 Put the raisins in a small bowl and pour over the Marsala. Let the raisins soak for approximately 1 hour until they are plump. Strain, reserving both the Marsala and the raisins.

2 Heat the olive oil in a large saucepan and cook the onions over a low heat for 15 minutes until golden and tender. Add the garlic and sage and cook for an additional minute. Add the tomatoes, cook for an additional 2–3 minutes then add the stock, vinegar and reserved Marsala. Bring to a boil, cover and simmer for 25 minutes.

3 Add the sardines to the stew and simmer gently for 2–3 minutes before adding the raisins, olives and pine nuts. Simmer for a final 2–3 minutes until the fish are cooked. Add the parsley and serve immediately.

VARIATION

Substitute Home-Salted Cod (see page 90) or smoked cod for the sardines.

Red Shrimp Curry

Serves 4

INGREDIENTS

2 tbsp. vegetable oil	1 small red chili, deseeded and	½ tsp. ground black pepper
1 garlic clove, finely chopped	finely sliced	2 garlic cloves, chopped
1 tbsp. red curry paste	10 leaves Thai basil, if available,	2 stalks lemon grass, chopped
scant 1 cup coconut milk	or ordinary basil	1 kaffir lime leaf, finely chopped
2 tbsp. Thai fish sauce		1 tsp. freshly grated ginger or
1 tsp. sugar	RED CURRY PASTE	galangal, if available
12 large raw shrimp, de-veined	3 dried long red chilies	1 tsp. shrimp paste (optional)
2 lime leaves, finely shredded	½ tsp. ground coriander	½ tsp. salt
	¼ tsp. ground cumin	

1 Make the red curry paste. Put all the ingredients in a blender or spice grinder and blend to a smooth paste, adding a little water if necessary. A mortar and pestle may also be used. Set aside.

2 Heat the oil in a wok or frying pan until almost smoking. Add the chopped garlic and fry until golden. Add 1 tablespoon of the curry paste and cook for an additional minute. Add half the coconut milk, the fish sauce, and the sugar. Stir well. The mixture should thicken a little.

3 Add the shrimp and simmer for 3–4 minutes until they turn color. Add the remaining coconut milk, the lime leaves and the chili. Cook an additional 2–3 minutes until the shrimp are just tender.

4 Add the basil leaves, stir until wilted and serve immediately.

COOK'S TIP

This recipe makes a little more curry paste than you need, but it keeps well. Stir a little into canned tuna with some chopped spring onion, lime juice and pinto beans for a delicious sandwich filling.

Curried Shrimp with Zucchini

Serves 4

INGREDIENTS

12 oz. small zucchini
1 tsp. salt
1 lb. cooked jumbo shrimp,
 peeled and de-veined
5 tbsp. vegetable oil
4 garlic cloves, finely chopped

5 tbsp. chopped cilantro
1 fresh green chili, deseeded and
 finely chopped
½ tsp. ground turmeric
1½ tsp. ground cumin
pinch cayenne pepper

7 oz. can chopped tomatoes
1 tsp. freshly grated ginger
1 tbsp. lemon juice
steamed basmati rice, to serve

1 Wash and trim the zucchini. Cut into small batons. Put into a colander and sprinkle with a little of the salt. Set aside for 30 minutes. Rinse, drain, and pat dry. Spread the shrimp on paper towels to drain.

2 In a wok or frying pan, heat the oil over a high heat. Add the garlic. As soon as the garlic begins to brown, add the zucchini, cilantro, green chili, turmeric, cumin, cayenne, tomatoes, ginger, lemon juice, and the remaining salt. Stir well and bring to a boil.

3 Cover and simmer over a low heat for about 5 minutes. Uncover and add the shrimp.

4 Increase the heat to high and simmer for about 5 minutes to reduce the liquid to a thick sauce. Serve immediately with steamed basmati rice, garnished with lime wedges.

VARIATION

If you can't find cooked jumbo shrimp for this recipe, use smaller cooked shrimp instead but these release quite a lot of liquid so you may need to increase the final simmering time to thicken the sauce.

Salads,
Summer & Dishes
Suppers

Fish is the perfect ingredient for a midweek supper because it cooks so quickly. It is also wonderful marinated and simply grilled or barbecued and makes a perfect ingredient in a salad, either warm or cold.

This chapter contains a variety of recipes designed to be simple but taste as if you have spent hours preparing them. There are substantial main course salads, like Tuna Bean Salad, Moroccan Couscous Salad, or Caesar Salad.

Quick suppers include the best Fish & Chips ever, plus Salmon Frittata and Tuna Fishcakes. Lots of barbecue ideas are here as well, including Barbecued Monkfish, Char-grilled Scallops, and Mixed Seafood Brochettes.

Caesar Salad

Serves 4

INGREDIENTS

1 large romaine lettuce or
 2 hearts of romaine
4 anchovies, drained and halved
 lengthwise
Parmesan shavings, to garnish

DRESSING
2 garlic cloves, crushed

1½ tsp. Dijon mustard
1 tsp. Worcestershire sauce
4 anchovies in olive oil, drained
 and chopped
1 egg yolk
1 tbsp. lemon juice
⅔ cup olive oil

4 tbsp. freshly grated
 Parmesan cheese
salt and pepper

CROUTONS
4 thick slices day-old bread
2 tbsp. olive oil
1 garlic clove, crushed

1 Make the dressing. In a food processor or blender, put the garlic, mustard, Worcestershire sauce, anchovies, egg yolk, lemon juice and seasoning and blend together for 30 seconds, until foaming. Add the olive oil, drop by drop until the mixture begins to thicken then in a steady stream until all the oil is incorporated. Scrape out of the food processor or blender. Add a little hot water if the dressing is too thick. Stir in the grated Parmesan cheese. Taste for seasoning and set aside in the refrigerator until required.

2 For the croutons, cut the bread into ½ in. cubes. Toss with the oil and garlic in a bowl. Transfer to a baking sheet in a single. Bake in a preheated oven at 350° F, for 15–20 minutes, stirring occasionally, until the croutons are browned and crisp. Remove from the oven and let cool.

3 Separate the romaine lettuce or hearts of romaine into individual leaves and wash. Tear into pieces and spin dry in a salad spinner. Alternatively, dry the leaves on clean paper towels. (Excess moisture will dilute the dressing and make the salad taste watery.) Transfer to a plastic bag and refrigerate until needed.

4 To assemble the salad, put the lettuce pieces into a large serving bowl. Add the dressing and toss thoroughly until all the leaves are coated. Top with the halved anchovies, croutons, and Parmesan shavings. Serve at once while still hot.

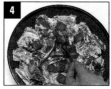

Moroccan Couscous Salad

Serves 4

INGREDIENTS

1 cup couscous	2 garlic cloves, finely chopped	4 scallions, sliced
1 cinnamon stick, about 2 in. long	½ tsp. ground turmeric	7 oz. can tuna in olive oil, drained and flaked
2 tsp. coriander seeds	pinch cayenne pepper	3 tbsp. chopped cilantro
1 tsp. cumin seeds	1 tbsp. lemon juice	salt and pepper
2 tbsp. olive oil	¼ cup golden raisins	
1 small onion, finely chopped	3 ripe plum tomatoes, chopped	
	½ cucumber, chopped	

1 Cook the couscous according to the packet instructions, omitting any butter recommended. Transfer to a large bowl and set aside.

2 Heat a small frying pan and add the cinnamon stick, coriander seeds, and cumin seeds. Cook over a high heat until the seeds begin to pop and smell fragrant. Remove from the heat and pour the seeds into a mortar. Grind with a pestle to a fine powder.

Alternatively, grind in a spice grinder. Set aside.

3 Heat the oil in a clean frying pan and add the onion. Cook over a low heat for 7–8 minutes until softened and lightly browned. Add the garlic and cook for an additional minute. Stir in the roasted and ground spices, turmeric, and cayenne and cook for an additional minute. Remove from the heat and stir in the lemon juice. Add this mixture to the couscous and

mix well together, ensuring that all of the grains are well coated.

4 Add the golden raisins, tomatoes, cucumber, scallions, tuna, and chopped coriander. Season with salt and pepper to taste and mix together. Allow to cool completely and serve at room temperature.

Tuna Niçoise Salad

Serves 4

INGREDIENTS

4 eggs	1 garlic clove, crushed	2 cups cucumber, peeled, cut
1 lb. new potatoes	1½ tsp. Dijon mustard	in half and sliced
1 cup dwarf green beans,	2 tsp. lemon juice	½ cup pitted black olives
trimmed and halved	2 tbsp. chopped fresh basil	1¾ oz. can anchovies in
2 x 6 oz. tuna steaks	2 baby lettuces	oil, drained
6 tbsp. olive oil, plus extra	1½ cups cherry tomatoes, halved	salt and pepper
for brushing		

1 Bring a small saucepan of water to a boil. Add the eggs and cook for 7–9 minutes from when the water returns to a boil—7 minutes for a slightly soft center, 9 minutes for a firm center. Drain and refresh under cold running water. Set aside.

2 Cook the potatoes in boiling salted water for 10–12 minutes until tender. Add the beans 3 minutes before the end of the cooking time. Drain both vegetables well and refresh under cold water. Drain well.

3 Wash and dry the tuna steaks. Brush with a little olive oil and season. Cook on a preheated ridged grill pan for 2–3 minutes each side, until just tender but still slightly pink in the center. Set aside to rest.

4 Whisk together the garlic, mustard, lemon juice, basil and seasoning. Whisk in the olive oil.

5 To assemble the salad, break apart the lettuces and tear into large pieces. Divide between individual

serving plates. Next add the potatoes and beans, tomatoes, cucumber and olives. Toss lightly together. Shell the eggs and cut into quarters lengthwise. Arrange these on top of the salad. Scatter over the anchovies.

6 Flake the tuna steaks and arrange on top of the salads. Pour over the dressing and serve.

VARIATION

Use 7 oz. cans of tuna in olive oil, drained and flaked, instead of the fresh tuna.

Tuna Bean Salad

Serves 4

INGREDIENTS

1 cup dried navy beans	1 small red onion, very finely	TO GARNISH
1 tbsp. lemon juice	sliced (optional)	parsley sprigs
5 tbsp. extra-virgin olive oil, plus	1 tbsp. chopped fresh parsley	lemon wedges
extra for brushing	4 x 6 oz. tuna steaks	
1 garlic clove, finely chopped	salt and pepper	

1 Soak the navy beans for 8 hours or overnight in at least twice their volume of cold water.

2 When you're ready to cook, drain the beans and place in a saucepan with twice their volume of fresh water. Bring slowly to a boil, skimming off any scum that rises to the surface. Boil the beans rapidly for 10 minutes, then reduce the heat and simmer for an additional 1¼–1½ hours until the beans are tender.

3 Meanwhile, mix together the lemon juice, olive oil, garlic, and seasoning. Drain the beans thoroughly and mix together with the olive oil mixture, onion and parsley. Season to taste and set aside.

4 Wash and dry the tuna steaks. Brush lightly with olive oil and season. Cook on a preheated ridged grill pan for 2 minutes on each side until just pink in the center.

5 Divide the bean salad between 4 serving plates. Top each with a tuna steak. Garnish with parsley sprigs and lemon wedges and serve immediately.

COOK'S TIP

You could use canned navy beans instead of dried. Reheat according to the instructions on the can, drain and toss with the dressing as above.

Thai Seafood Salad

Serves 4

INGREDIENTS

1 lb. live mussels
8 raw jumbo shrimp
12 oz. squid, cleaned and sliced
    widthwise into rings
4 oz. cooked peeled shrimp
½ red onion, finely sliced
½ red bell pepper, deseeded and
    finely sliced

1 cup beansprouts
2 cups shredded bok choi

DRESSING
1 garlic clove, crushed
1 tsp. grated fresh ginger root
1 red chili, deseeded and
    finely chopped

2 tbsp. chopped fresh cilantro
1 tbsp. lime juice
1 tsp. finely grated lime rind
1 tbsp. light soy sauce
5 tbsp. sunflower or peanut oil
2 tsp. sesame oil
salt and pepper

1 Prepare the mussels by scrubbing or scraping the shells and removing any beards. Place in a large saucepan with just the water that clings to their shells. Cook over a high heat for 3–4 minutes, shaking the pan occasionally, until all the mussels have opened. Discard any that remain closed. Strain the mussels, reserving the poaching liquid, and refresh the mussels under cold water. Drain again and set aside.

2 Bring the reserved poaching liquid to a boil and add the tiger shrimp. Simmer for 5 minutes. Add the squid and cook for an additional 2 minutes until both the shrimp and squid are cooked through. Remove them with a slotted spoon and plunge them immediately into a large bowl of cold water. Reserve the poaching liquid. Drain the shrimp and squid again.

3 Shell the mussels and put into a bowl with the tiger shrimp, squid and shrimp. Refrigerate for 1 hour.

4 For the dressing, put all the ingredients, except the oils, into a blender or spice grinder and blend to a smooth paste. Add the oils, reserved poaching liquid, seasoning and 4 tbsp. cold water. Blend again.

5 Just before serving, combine the onion, red bell pepper, beansprouts, and bok choi in a bowl and toss with 2–3 tbsp. of the dressing. Arrange the vegetables on a large serving plate or in a bowl. Toss the remaining dressing with the seafood and add to the vegetables.

Skate & Spinach Salad

Serves 4

INGREDIENTS

1 lb. 9 oz. skate wings, trimmed
2 sprigs fresh rosemary
1 fresh bay leaf
1 tbsp. black peppercorns
1 lemon, quartered
1 lb. baby spinach leaves

1 tbsp. olive oil
1 small red onion, thinly sliced
2 garlic cloves, crushed
½ tsp. chili flakes
½ cup pine nuts, lightly toasted
½ cup raisins

1 tbsp. light brown sugar
salt and pepper
2 tbsp. chopped fresh parsley,
   to garnish

1 Put the skate wings into a large saucepan with the rosemary, bay leaf, peppercorns, and lemon quarters. Cover with cold water and bring to a boil. Simmer, covered, for 4–5 minutes until the flesh begins to come away from the cartilage. Remove the pan from the heat and let stand for 15 minutes.

2 Lift the fish from the poaching water and remove the flesh from the fish in shreds. Set aside.

3 Meanwhile, in a clean saucepan, cook the spinach with just the water that clings to the leaves after washing, over a high heat for 30 seconds until just wilted. Drain, refresh under cold water and drain well once more. Squeeze out any excess water and set aside.

4 Heat the olive oil in a large, deep frying pan. Add the red onion and fry for 3–4 minutes until softened but not browned. Add the garlic, chili flakes, pine nuts, raisins, and sugar. Cook for 1–2 minutes, then add the spinach. Toss for 1 minute until heated through.

5 Gently fold in the skate and cook for an additional minute. Season to taste with salt and pepper.

6 Divide the salad between 4 serving plates and sprinkle with the chopped parsley. Serve immediately.

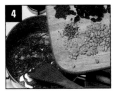

Grilled Red Mullet

Serves 4

INGREDIENTS

1 lemon, thinly sliced	SAUTE POTATOES AND SHALLOTS	DRESSING
2 garlic cloves, crushed	4 tbsp. olive oil	4 tbsp. olive oil
4 sprigs fresh flat-leaf parsley	2 lb. potatoes, diced	1 tbsp. lemon juice
4 sprigs fresh thyme	8 whole garlic cloves, unpeeled	1 tbsp. chopped fresh
8 leaves fresh sage	12 small whole shallots	flat-leaf parsley
2 large shallots, sliced		1 tbsp. chopped fresh chives
8 small red mullet, cleaned		salt and pepper
8 slices prosciutto		
salt and pepper		

1 For the sauté potatoes and shallots, heat the olive oil in a large frying pan and add the potatoes, garlic cloves, and shallots. Cook gently, stirring regularly, for 12–15 minutes until golden, crisp and tender.

2 Meanwhile, divide the lemon slices, halved if necessary, garlic, parsley, thyme, sage, and shallots between the cavities of the fish. Season well. Wrap a slice of prosciutto around each fish. Secure in place with a toothpick.

3 Arrange fish on a broiler pan and cook under a preheated hot broiler for 5–6 minutes on each side until tender.

4 To make the dressing, mix together the oil and lemon juice with the finely chopped parsley and chives. Season to taste.

5 Divide the potatoes and shallots between 4 serving plates and top each with the fish. Drizzle the dressing over the 4 dishes and serve immediately.

Poached Rainbow Trout

Serves 4

INGREDIENTS

4 x 12 oz. rainbow trout, cleaned
1 lb. 9 oz. new potatoes
3 scallions, finely chopped
1 egg, hard-cooked and chopped

COURT-BOUILLON
3¾ cups cold water
3¾ cups dry white wine
3 tbsp. white wine vinegar

2 large carrots, roughly chopped
1 onion, roughly chopped
2 celery stalks, roughly chopped
2 leeks, roughly chopped
2 garlic cloves, roughly chopped
2 fresh bay leaves
4 sprigs fresh parsley
4 sprigs fresh thyme
6 black peppercorns
1 tsp. salt

WATERCRESS MAYONNAISE
1 egg yolk
1 tsp. Dijon mustard
1 tsp. white wine vinegar
2 oz. watercress leaves, chopped
1 cup light olive oil
salt and pepper

TO GARNISH
lemon slices
flat-leaf parsley

1 First make the court-bouillon. Place all the ingredients in a large saucepan and bring slowly to a boil. Cover and simmer gently for about 30 minutes. Strain the liquid through a fine sieve into a clean pan. Bring to a boil again and simmer fast, uncovered, for 15–20 minutes until the court-bouillon is reduced to 2½ cups.

2 Place the trout in a large frying pan. Add the court-bouillon and bring slowly to a boil. Remove from the heat and leave the fish in the poaching liquid to go cold.

3 Meanwhile, make the watercress mayonnaise. Put the egg yolk, mustard, wine vinegar, watercress, and seasoning into a food processor or blender and blend for 30 seconds until foaming. Begin adding the olive oil, drop by drop, until the mixture begins to thicken. Continue adding the oil in a slow stream until it is all incorporated. Add a little hot water if the mixture seems too thick. Season to taste and set aside.

4 Cook the potatoes in plenty of boiling salted water for 12–15 minutes until soft and tender. Drain well and refresh them under cold running water. Set the potatoes aside until cold.

5 When the potatoes are cold, cut them in half if they are very large, and toss thoroughly with the watercress mayonnaise, finely chopped scallions, and hard-cooked egg.

6 Carefully lift the fish from the poaching liquid and drain on paper towels. Carefully pull the skin away from each of the trout, garnish, and serve immediately with the potato salad.

Baked Salmon

Serves 8–10

INGREDIENTS

6 lb. 8 oz. salmon filleted
8 tbsp. chopped mixed herbs
2 tbsp. green peppercorns in
   brine, drained
1 tsp. finely grated lime rind
6 tbsp. dry vermouth or dry
   white wine
salt and pepper
parsley sprigs, to garnish

RED BELL PEPPER RELISH
½ cup white wine vinegar
¼ cups light olive oil
1–2 tsp. chili sauce, to taste
6 scallions, finely sliced
1 orange or red bell pepper,
   deseeded and finely diced
1 tbsp. chopped fresh
   flat-leaf parsley
2 tbsp. chopped fresh chives

CAPER AND GHERKIN
   MAYONNAISE
1½ cups good-quality mayonnaise
3 tbsp. chopped capers
3 tbsp. finely chopped gherkins
2 tbsp. chopped fresh
   flat-leaf parsley
1 tbsp. Dijon mustard

1 Wash and dry the salmon fillets and place one fillet, skin side down, on a large sheet of oiled foil. Mix together the herbs, peppercorns and lime rind and spread over the top. Season well and lay the second fillet on top, skin side up. Drizzle over the vermouth or white wine. Wrap the foil over the salmon, twisting well to make a loose but tightly sealed parcel.

2 Transfer the foil parcel to a large baking sheet and bake in a preheated oven at 250° F, for 1½ hours until tender. Remove from the oven and allow to rest for 20 minutes before serving.

3 Meanwhile, make the red bell pepper relish.

Whisk together the vinegar, olive oil, and chili sauce to taste. Add the scallions, red bell pepper, parsley and chives. Season and set aside.

4 To make the caper and gherkin mayonnaise, mix all the ingredients together and set aside.

5 Unwrap the cooked salmon and slice thickly. Arrange the slices on a large serving platter and serve with the red bell pepper relish and caper and gherkin mayonnaise. Garnish with fresh parsley sprigs.

Barbecued Monkfish

Serves 4

INGREDIENTS

4 tbsp. olive oil
grated rind of 1 lime
2 tsp. Thai fish sauce
2 garlic cloves, crushed

1 tsp. grated fresh ginger root
2 tbsp. chopped fresh basil
1 lb. 9 oz. monkfish fillet,
    cut into chunks

2 limes, each cut into 6 wedges
salt and pepper

1 Mix together the olive oil, lime rind, fish sauce, garlic, ginger, and basil. Season and set aside.

2 Wash and dry the fish. Add to the marinade and mix well. Marinate for about 2 hours, stirring occasionally.

3 If you are using bamboo skewers, soak them in cold water for 30 minutes. Then, lift the monkfish pieces from the marinade and thread them on to the skewers, alternating with the lime wedges.

4 Transfer the skewers, either to a lit barbecue or to a preheated ridged grill pan. Cook for 5–6 minutes, turning regularly, until the fish is tender. Serve the skewers immediately.

VARIATION

You could use any type of white fish for this recipe but sprinkle the pieces with salt and leave for 2 hours to firm the flesh, before rinsing, drying, and then adding to the marinade.

Cod & French Fries

Serves 4

INGREDIENTS

	BATTER	MAYONNAISE	TO GARNISH
2 lb. old potatoes	½ oz. fresh yeast	1 egg yolk	lemon wedges
4 x 6 oz. thick pieces cod	1¼ cups beer	1 tsp. wholegrain mustard	parsley sprigs
fillet, head end	2 cups all-purpose flour	1 tbsp. lemon juice	
vegetable oil, for	2 tsp. salt	1 cup light olive oil	
deep-frying		salt and pepper	
salt and pepper			

1 For the batter, cream the yeast with a little of the beer to a smooth paste. Gradually stir in the rest of the beer. Sift the all-purpose flour and salt into a bowl, make a well in the center and add the yeast mixture. Gradually whisk to a smooth batter. Cover and leave at room temperature for 1 hour.

2 For the mayonnaise, put the egg yolk, mustard, lemon juice, and seasoning into a food processor. Blend for 30 seconds until frothy. Begin adding the olive oil, drop by drop, until the

mixture begins to thicken. Continue adding the oil in a slow, steady stream until all the oil has been incorporated. Taste for seasoning. Thin with a little hot water if the mayonnaise is too thick. Refrigerate until needed.

3 For the French fries, cut the potatoes into slices about ½ inch thick. Heat a large pan, half-filled with vegetable oil, to 275° F or until a cube of bread browns in 1 minute. Cook the French fries in 2 batches for about 5 minutes, until they are cooked through but not browned. Place on paper towels to drain and set aside.

4 Increase the heat to 325° F or until a cube of bread browns in 45 seconds. Season the fish then dip into the batter. Fry 2 pieces at a

time for 7–8 minutes until deep golden brown and cooked through. Drain on paper towels and keep warm while you cook the remaining fish. Keep these warm while you finish cooking the French fries.

5 Increase the heat to 375° F or until a cube of bread browns in 30 seconds. Cook the French Fries again, in 2 batches, for 2–3 minutes until crisp and golden. Drain on waxed paper and sprinkle with salt.

6 Serve the fish with the French fries and mayonnaise. Serve while still hot, garnished with lemon wedges and parsley sprigs.

Haddock Goujons

Serves 4

INGREDIENTS

6 oz. herb focaccia bread	TARTAR SAUCE	2 tsp. chopped fresh chives
1 lb. 9 oz. skinless, boneless haddock fillet	1 egg yolk	2 tsp. chopped fresh parsley
2–3 tbsp. all-purpose flour	1 tsp. Dijon mustard	salt and pepper
2 eggs, lightly beaten	2 tsp. white wine vinegar	
vegetable oil, for deep-frying	⅔ cup light olive oil	
lemon wedges, to serve	1 tsp. finely chopped green olives	
parsley sprigs, to garnish	1 tsp. finely chopped gherkins	
	1 tsp. finely chopped capers	

1 Put the focaccia into the bowl of a food processor and blend to fine crumbs, then set aside. Slice the haddock fillet widthwise into fingers. Put the flour, egg, and breadcrumbs into separate bowls.

2 Dip the haddock fingers into the flour, then the egg, and the breadcrumbs to coat. Lay on a plate and refrigerate for 30 minutes. For the tartar sauce, put the egg yolk, mustard, vinegar, and seasoning into the bowl

of a food processor. Blend for 30 seconds until frothy. Begin adding the olive oil, drop by drop, until the mixture begins to thicken. Continue adding the olive oil in a slow, steady stream until all the oil is incorporated.

3 Scrape the tartar sauce from the food processor into a small mixing bowl and stir in the olives, gherkins, capers, chives, and parsley. Check for seasoning. Add a little hot water if the sauce is too thick.

4 Heat a large pan half filled with vegetable oil to 375° F or until a cube of bread browns in 30 seconds. Cook the haddock goujons, in batches of 3 or 4, for 3–4 minutes until the crumbs are browned and crisp and the fish is cooked. Drain on the kitchen paper and keep warm while you cook the remaining fish.

5 Serve the haddock goujons immediately, with the tartar sauce and lemon wedges.

Swordfish Steaks

Serves 4

INGREDIENTS

4 swordfish steaks, about
5½ oz. each
4 tbsp. olive oil
1 garlic clove, crushed
1 tsp. lemon rind
lemon wedges, to garnish

SALSA VERDE
1 cup flat-leaf parsley leaves
½ cup mixed herbs, such as basil,
mint, chives
1 garlic clove, chopped
1 tbsp. capers, drained and rinsed

1 tbsp. green peppercorns in
brine, drained
4 anchovies in oil, drained and
roughly chopped
1 tsp. Dijon mustard
½ cup extra-virgin olive oil
salt and pepper

1 Wash and dry the swordfish steaks and arrange in a nonmetallic dish. Mix together the olive oil, garlic, and lemon rind. Pour over the swordfish steaks and leave to marinate for 2 hours.

2 For the salsa verde, put the parsley leaves, mixed herbs, garlic, capers, green peppercorns, anchovies, mustard, and olive oil into a food processor or blender.

Blend to a smooth paste, adding a little warm water if necessary. Season to taste and set aside.

3 Remove the swordfish steaks from the marinade. Cook on a barbecue or preheated ridged grill pan for 2–3 minutes each side until tender. Serve immediately with the salsa verde and lemon wedges.

VARIATIONS

*Any firm-fleshed fish
will do this recipe.
Try tuna or even
shark instead.*

Swordfish or Tuna Fajitas

Serves 4

INGREDIENTS

3 tbsp. olive oil

2 tsp. chili powder

1 tsp. ground cumin

pinch cayenne pepper

1 garlic clove, crushed

2 lb. swordfish or tuna

1 red bell pepper, deseeded and thinly sliced

1 yellow bell pepper, deseeded and thinly sliced

2 zucchini, cut into batons

1 large onion, thinly sliced

12 soft flour tortillas

1 tbsp. lemon juice

3 tbsp. chopped cilantro

salt and pepper

²⁄₃ cup sour cream, to serve

GUACAMOLE

1 large avocado

1 tomato, skinned, deseeded and diced

1 garlic clove, crushed

dash Tabasco

2 tbsp. lemon juice

salt and pepper

1 Mix together the oil, chili powder, cumin, cayenne, and garlic. Cut the swordfish or tuna into chunks and mix with the marinade. Set aside for 1–2 hours.

2 Heat a large frying pan until hot. Add the fish and its marinade to the pan and cook for 2 minutes, stirring occasionally, until the

fish begins to brown. Add the red bell pepper, yellow bell pepper, zucchini, and onion and continue cooking for a further 5 minutes until the vegetables have softened but still firm.

3 Meanwhile, warm the tortillas in a low oven or microwave according to the packet instructions.

4 To make the guacamole, mash the avocado until fairly smooth, stir in the tomato, garlic, Tabasco, lemon juice, seasoning.

5 Add the lemon juice, cilantro, and seasoning to the vegetable mix. Spoon some of the mixture down the warmed tortilla. Top with guacamole and a spoonful of sour cream and roll up.

Smoked Fish Pie

Serves 6

INGREDIENTS

2 tbsp. olive oil	12 oz. skinless, boneless white	1 tsp. mustard powder
1 onion, finely chopped	fish such as haddock, hake or	2½ cups milk
1 leek, thinly sliced	monkfish, cubed	½ cup Gruyère cheese, grated
1 carrot, diced	8 oz. cooked peeled shrimp	
1 celery stalk, diced	2 tbsp. chopped fresh parsley	TOPPING
½ cup button mushrooms, halved	1 tbsp. chopped fresh dill	1½ lb. potatoes, unpeeled
grated rind 1 lemon		¼ cup butter, melted
12 oz. skinless, boneless smoked	SAUCE	1 oz. Gruyère cheese, grated
cod or haddock fillet, cubed	2 tbsp. butter	salt and pepper
	⅓ cup all-purpose flour	

1 For the sauce, heat the butter in a large saucepan and when melted, add the flour and mustard powder. Stir until smooth and cook over a very low heat for 2 minutes without coloring. Slowly beat in the milk until smooth. Simmer gently for 2 minutes then stir in the cheese until smooth. Remove from the heat and put some plastic wrap over the surface of the sauce to prevent a skin forming. Set aside.

2 Meanwhile, for the topping, boil the whole potatoes in plenty of salted water for 15 minutes. Drain well and set aside until cool enough to handle.

3 Heat the olive oil in a clean pan and add the onion. Cook for 5 minutes until softened. Add the leek, carrot, celery, and mushrooms and cook an additional 10 minutes until the vegetables have softened. Stir in the lemon rind and cook briefly.

4 Add the softened vegetables with the fish, shrimp, parsley, and dill to the sauce. Season with salt and pepper and transfer to a greased casserole dish.

5 Peel the cooled potatoes and grate coarsely. Mix with the melted butter. Cover the filling with the grated potato and sprinkle with the grated Gruyère cheese.

6 Cover loosely with foil and bake in a preheated oven at 400° F, for 30 minutes. Remove the foil and bake an additional 30 minutes until the topping is tender and golden and the filling is bubbling. Serve immediately with your favorite selection of vegetables.

Hake Steaks
with Chermoula

Serves 4

INGREDIENTS

4 hake steaks, about 8 oz. each
½ cup pitted green olives

MARINADE
6 tbsp. finely chopped cilantro
6 tbsp. finely chopped
    fresh parsley
6 garlic cloves, crushed
1 tbsp. ground cumin

1 tsp. ground coriander
1 tbsp. paprika
pinch cayenne pepper
⅔ cup fresh lemon juice
1¼ cups olive oil

1 For the marinade, mix together the cilantro, parsley, garlic, cumin, coriander, paprika, cayenne, lemon juice, olive oil.

2 Wash and dry the hake steaks and place in an ovenproof dish. Pour the marinade over the fish and leave for at least 1 hour and preferably overnight.

3 Before cooking, scatter the olives over the fish. Cover the dish with foil.

4 Cook in a preheated oven at 325° F. Cook for 35–40 minutes until the fish is tender. Serve with freshly cooked vegetables.

VARIATION

Remove the fish from the marinade and dust with seasoned flour. Fry in oil or clarified butter until golden. Warm through the marinade, but do not boil, and serve as a sauce with lemon slices.

Stuffed Mackerel

Serves 4

INGREDIENTS

4 large mackerel, cleaned
1 tbsp. olive oil
1 small onion, finely sliced

1 tsp. ground cinnamon
½ ground ginger
2 tbsp. raisins

2 tbsp. pine nuts, toasted
8 grape leaves in brine, drained
salt and pepper

1 Wash and dry the fish and set aside. Heat the oil in a small frying pan and add the onion. Cook gently for 5 minutes until softened. Add the cinnamon and ginger and then cook for 30 seconds before adding the raisins and pine nuts. Remove from the heat and allow to cool.

2 Stuff each of the fish with a quarter of the stuffing mixture. Wrap each fish in 2 vine leaves, securing with toothpicks.

3 Cook on a preheated barbecue or ridged grill pan for 5 minutes on each side until the vine leaves have scorched and the fish is tender. Serve immediately.

VARIATION

This stuffing works equally well with many other fish, including sea bass and red mullet.

Tuna Fishcakes

Serves 4

INGREDIENTS

8 oz. potatoes, cubed

1 tbsp. olive oil

1 large shallot, finely chopped

1 garlic clove, finely chopped

1 tsp. thyme leaves

2 x 7 oz. cans tuna in olive oil, drained

grated rind ½ lemon

1 tbsp. chopped fresh parsley

2–3 tbsp. all-purpose flour

1 egg, lightly beaten

4 oz. fresh breadcrumbs

vegetable oil, for shallow frying

salt and pepper

QUICK TOMATO SAUCE

2 tbsp. olive oil

14 oz. can chopped tomatoes

1 garlic clove, crushed

½ tsp. sugar

grated rind ½ lemon

1 tbsp. chopped fresh basil

salt and pepper

1 For the tuna fishcakes, cook the potatoes in plenty of boiling salted water for 12–15 minutes until tender. Mash, leaving a few lumps, and set aside.

2 Heat the oil in a small frying pan and cook the shallot gently for 5 minutes until softened. Add the garlic and thyme leaves and cook for an additional minute. Allow to cool slightly then add to the potatoes with the tuna, lemon rind, parsley, and seasoning. Mix together well but leave some texture.

3 Form the mixture into 6–8 cakes. Dip the cakes first in the flour, then the egg and finally the breadcrumbs to coat. Refrigerate for 30 minutes.

4 Meanwhile, make the tomato sauce. Put the olive oil, tomatoes, garlic, sugar, lemon rind, basil, and seasoning into a saucepan and bring to a boil. Cover and simmer gently for 30 minutes. Uncover and simmer for an additional 15 minutes until thickened.

5 Heat enough oil in a frying pan to generously cover the bottom. When hot, add the fishcakes in batches and fry for 3–4 minutes each side until golden and crisp. Drain on paper towels while you fry the remaining fishcakes. Serve them hot with the tomato sauce.

Sardines with Pesto

Serves 4

INGREDIENTS

16 large sardines, cleaned,
   scaled and gutted
2 cups loosely packed fresh
   basil leaves
2 garlic cloves, crushed
2 tbsp. pine nuts, toasted

½ cup freshly grated
   Parmesan cheese
⅔ cup olive oil
salt and pepper
lemon wedges, to serve

1 Wash and dry the sardines and arrange on a broiler pan.

2 Put the basil leaves, garlic, and pine nuts in a food processor. Blend until finely chopped. Scrape out of the food processor and stir in the Parmesan and oil. Season with salt and pepper to taste.

3 Spread a little of the pesto over one side of the sardines and place under a preheated hot broiler for 3 minutes. Turn the fish, spread with more pesto, and broil for an additional 3 minutes until the sardines are cooked.

4 Serve with extra pesto and lemon wedges.

VARIATION

This treatment will also work well with other small oily fish such as herrings and pilchards.

Salmon Frittata

Serves 6

INGREDIENTS

9 oz. skinless, boneless salmon
3 sprigs fresh thyme
sprig fresh parsley plus 2 tbsp.
   chopped fresh parsley
5 black peppercorns
½ small onion, sliced
½ stalk celery, sliced
½ carrot, chopped

6 oz. asparagus spears, chopped
3 oz. baby carrots, halved
¼ cup butter
1 large onion, finely sliced
1 garlic clove, finely chopped
1 cup peas, fresh or frozen
8 eggs, lightly beaten
1 tbsp. chopped fresh dill

salt and pepper
lemon wedges, to garnish

TO SERVE
crème fraîche
salad leaves
crusty bread

1 Place the salmon in a saucepan with one sprig of the thyme, the parsley sprig, peppercorns, onion, celery, and carrot. Cover the vegetables and fish with cold water and bring slowly to a boil. Remove the saucepan from the heat and leave to stand for 5 minutes.
Lift the fish out of the the poaching liquid, flake the flesh and set aside. Discard the poaching liquid.

2 Bring a large saucepan of salted water to a boil and blanch the asparagus for 2 minutes. Drain and refresh under the cold water. Blanch the carrots for 4 minutes. Drain and refresh under cold water. Drain again and pat dry. Set aside.

3 Heat half the butter in a large frying pan and add the onion. Cook gently for 8–10 minutes until softened but not colored. Add the garlic and remaining sprigs

of thyme and cook for an additional minute. Add the asparagus, carrots and peas and heat through. Remove from the heat.

4 Add the vegetables to the eggs with the chopped parsley, dill, salmon, and seasoning and stir briefly. Heat the remaining butter in the pan and return the mixture to the pan. Cover and cook over a low heat for 10 minutes.

5 Cook under a preheated medium broiler for an additional 5 minutes until set and golden. Serve hot or cold in wedges topped with a dollop of crème fraîche, salad and crusty bread. Garnish with lemon wedges.

Mixed Seafood Brochettes

Serves 4

INGREDIENTS

8 oz. skinless, boneless
turbot fillet

8 oz. skinless, boneless
salmon fillet

8 scallops

8 large jumbo shrimp or
langoustines

16 fresh bay leaves

1 lemon, sliced

4 tbsp. olive oil

grated rind 1 lemon

4 tbsp. chopped mixed herbs
such as thyme, parsley,
chives, basil

black pepper

LEMON BUTTER RICE

2 cups long-grain rice

grated rind and juice 1 lemon

¼ cup butter

salt and pepper

TO GARNISH

lemon wedges

dill sprigs

1 Chop the turbot and salmon into 8 pieces each. Thread on to 8 skewers, with the scallops and jumbo shrimp or langoustines, alternating with the bay leaves and lemon slices. Put into a nonmetallic dish in a single layer if possible.

2 Mix together the olive oil, lemon rind, herbs, and black pepper. Pour this over the fish. Cover and leave to marinate for 2 hours, turning once or twice.

3 For the lemon butter rice, bring a large pan of salted water to a boil and add the rice and lemon rind. Return to a boil and simmer for 7–8 minutes until the rice is tender. Drain well and immediately stir in the lemon juice and butter. Season with salt and pepper to taste.

4 Meanwhile, lift the fish brochettes from their marinade and cook on a lit barbecue or under a preheated hot broiler for 8–10 minutes, turning regularly, until cooked through. Serve with lemon butter rice. Garnish with lemon wedges and dill.

Char-Grilled Scallops

Serves 4

INGREDIENTS

16 king scallops	BEJEWELED COUSCOUS	3 scallions, finely chopped
3 tbsp. olive oil	2 cups couscous	1 tbsp. lime juice
grated rind 1 lime	½ yellow bell pepper, deseeded	2 tbsp. shredded fresh basil
2 tbsp. chopped fresh basil	and halved	salt and pepper
2 tbsp. chopped fresh chives	½ red bell pepper, deseeded	
1 garlic clove, finely chopped	and halved	TO GARNISH
black pepper	4 tbsp. extra-virgin olive oil	basil leaves
	1 small cucumber, chopped into	lime wedges
	½ inch pieces	

1 Clean and trim the scallops as necessary. Put into a nonmetallic dish. Mix together the olive oil, lime rind, basil, chives, garlic, and black pepper. Pour over the scallops and cover. Leave to marinate for 2 hours.

2 Cook the couscous according to the packet instructions, omitting any butter recommended. Brush the red and yellow bell pepper halves with a little of the olive oil and place under a preheated hot broiler for 5–6 minutes, turning once, until the skins are blackened and the flesh is tender. Put into a plastic bag and leave until cool enough to handle. When cool, peel off the skins and chop the flesh into ½ inch pieces. Add to the couscous with the remaining olive oil, cucumber, scallions, lemon juice, and seasoning. Set aside.

3 Lift the scallops from the marinade and thread on to 4 skewers. Cook on a lit barbecue or preheated ridged griddle for 1 minute on each side, until charred and firm but not quite cooked through. Remove from the heat and allow to rest for 2 minutes.

4 Stir the shredded basil into the couscous and divide on to plates. Put a skewer on each, garnish with basil leaves and lime wedges.

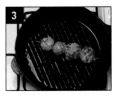

Shrimp Rostis

Serves 4

INGREDIENTS

12 oz. potatoes
12 oz. celeriac
1 carrot
½ small onion
8 oz. cooked peeled shrimp,
    thawed if frozen and well-
    drained on paper towels
¼ cup all-purpose flour
1 egg, lightly beaten

vegetable oil, for frying
salt and pepper

CHERRY TOMATO SALSA
8 oz. mixed cherry tomatoes such
    as baby plum, yellow, orange,
    pear, quartered
½ small mango, finely diced

1 red chili, deseeded and
    finely chopped
½ small red onion, finely chopped
1 tbsp. chopped cilantro
1 tbsp. chopped fresh chives
2 tbsp. olive oil
2 tsp. lemon juice
salt and pepper

1 For the salsa, mix together the tomatoes, mango, chili, red onion, cilantro, chives, olive oil, lemon juice, and seasoning. Set aside for the flavors to infuse.

2 Using a food processor or the fine blade of a box grater, finely grate the potatoes, celeriac, carrot and onion. Mix together with the shrimp, flour, and egg. Season well and set aside.

3 Divide the shrimp mixture into 8 equal pieces. Press each into a greased 4 inch cutter (if you only have one cutter, simply shape the rostis individually).

4 In a large frying pan, heat a shallow layer of shrimp oil. When hot, transfer the vegetable cakes, still in the cutters, to the frying pan, in batches if necessary. When the oil sizzles underneath, remove the cutter. Fry gently, pressing down with a spatula, for 6–8 minutes on each side, until crisp and browned and the vegetables are tender. Drain on paper towels. Serve immediately while still hot with the tomato salsa.

Moules Marinières

Serves 4

INGREDIENTS

2 lb. live mussels
2 shallots, finely chopped
2 garlic cloves, finely chopped
⅔ cup dry white wine
2 tbsp. chopped fresh parsley
salt and pepper

FRENCH FRIES
2 lb. potatoes
vegetable oil, for deep-frying
salt, to taste

TO SERVE (OPTIONAL)
lemon wedges
mayonnaise

1 Clean the mussels by scrubbing or scraping the shells and pulling out any beards. Discard any mussels with broken shells or that refuse to close when tapped sharply.

2 For the French fries, cut the potatoes into thin strips, about ½ inch thick. Fill a large pan or deep-fat fryer about one third full of vegetable oil and heat to 275° F or until a cube of bread browns in 1 minute. Add the chips in 3 batches and cook for 5–6 minutes until the chips are tender but not browned. Drain on paper towels.

3 Put the mussels in a large saucepan with the shallots, garlic and white wine. Cook, covered, over a high heat for 3–4 minutes until all the mussels have opened. Discard any mussels that remain closed. Add the parsley and taste for seasoning. Keep warm while you finish the fries.

4 Increase the temperature of the oil to 375° F, or until a cube of bread browns in 30 seconds. Cook the chips, again in 3 batches, for 2–3 minutes until golden and crisp. Drain on paper towels and sprinkle with salt.

5 Divide the mussels between 4 large serving bowls. Divide the chips between smaller bowls or plates and serve with lemon wedges and plenty of mayonnaise for dipping chips, if desired.

Provençal Mussels

Serves 4

INGREDIENTS

2 lb. live mussels

3 tbsp. olive oil

1 onion, finely chopped

3 garlic cloves, finely chopped

2 tsp. fresh thyme leaves

⅔ cup red wine

2 x 14 oz. cans chopped tomatoes

2 tbsp. chopped fresh parsley

salt and pepper

crusty bread, to serve

1 Clean the mussels by scrubbing or scraping the shells and pulling out any beards. Discard any mussels with broken shells or that do not close when tapped sharply. Put the mussels in a large saucepan with just the water that clings to their shells. Cook, covered, over a high heat for 3–4 minutes until all the mussels have opened. Discard any mussels that remain closed. Drain, reserving the cooking liquid. Set aside.

2 Heat the oil in a large saucepan and add the onion. Cook gently for 8–10 minutes until softened, but not colored. Add the garlic and thyme and cook for an additional 1 minute. Add the red wine and simmer rapidly until reduced and syrupy. Add the tomatoes and strained, reserved mussel cooking liquid and bring to a boil. Cover and simmer for 30 minutes. Uncover and cook for 15 minutes.

3 Add the mussels and cook for an additional 5 minutes until heated through. Stir in the parsley, season to taste and serve with plenty of fresh crusty bread.

VARIATION

Replace the mussels with an equal quantity of clams.

Pasta, Rice & other Grains

Nutritionists today recommend a diet high in complex carbohydrates, which include pasta, rice, potatoes, breads, and grains. A diet based around this food group ensures high energy levels without any dips in blood sugar levels, which can lead to bingeing.

This chapter includes a variety of dishes based on these foods. The most popular of these has to be pasta and there are a number of pasta dishes here. There are also a variety of skill levels represented, from very simple pasta dishes, like Spaghettini with Crab and Linguini with Sardines, to more complicated dishes, like homemade Squid Ink Pasta, Fideua, and Seafood Lasagna.

There are also pies and pasties, such as Herring and Potato Pie and Fish Pasties, as well as rice dishes, including Jambalaya, Lobster Risotto, and Shrimp & Asparagus Risotto.

Dishes using other grains include Buckwheat Pancakes with Smoked Salmon & Crème Fraîche, Fish & Bread Soup, and Pizza Marinara.

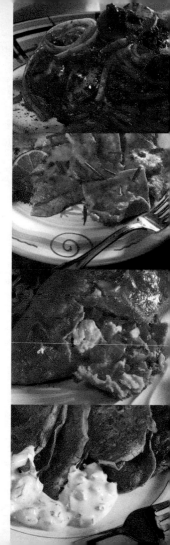

Tagliatelle with Broccoli & Anchovies

Serves 4

INGREDIENTS

6 tbsp. olive oil
½ cup fresh white breadcrumbs
1 lb. broccoli, cut into
    small florets
12 oz. dried tagliatelle

4 anchovy fillets, drained
    and chopped
2 garlic cloves, sliced
grated rind 1 lemon
large pinch chili flakes

salt and pepper
freshly grated Parmesan cheese,
    to serve

1 Heat 2 tablespoons of the olive oil in a frying pan and add the breadcrumbs. Stir-fry over a medium heat for 4–5 minutes until golden and crisp. Drain on paper towels.

2 Bring a large pan of salted water to a boil and add the broccoli. Blanch for 3 minutes then drain, reserving the water. Refresh the broccoli under cold water and drain again. Pat dry on paper towels and set the broccoli aside.

3 Bring the water back to a boil and add the tagliatelle. Cook according to the packet instructions until tender but still firm to the bite.

4 Meanwhile, heat another 2 tablespoons of the oil in a large frying pan or wok and add the anchovies. Cook for a minute then mash with a wooden spoon to a paste. Add the garlic, lemon rind, and chili flakes and cook gently for 2 minutes.

Add the broccoli and cook for an additional 3–4 minutes until hot.

5 Drain the cooked pasta and add to the broccoli mixture with the remaining 2 tbsp. olive oil and seasoning. Toss together well.

6 Divide the tagliatelle between serving plates. Top with the fried breadcrumbs and Parmesan cheese and serve immediately.

Pasta Puttanesca

Serves 4

INGREDIENTS

3 tbsp. extra-virgin olive oil
1 large red onion, finely chopped
4 anchovy fillets, drained
pinch chili flakes
2 garlic cloves, finely chopped
14 oz. can chopped tomatoes

2 tbsp. tomato paste
8 oz. dried spaghetti
½ cup pitted black olives,
    roughly chopped
½ cup pitted green olives,
    roughly chopped

1 tbsp. capers, drained
    and rinsed
4 sun-dried tomatoes,
    roughly chopped
salt and pepper

1 Heat the oil in a saucepan and add the onion, anchovies, and chili flakes. Cook for 10 minutes until softened and starting to brown. Add the garlic and cook for 30 seconds.

2 Add the tomatoes and tomato paste and bring to a boil. Simmer gently for 10 minutes.

3 Meanwhile, cook the spaghetti in plenty of boiling salted water according to the packet instructions until tender but still firm to the bite.

4 Add the olives, capers, and sun-dried tomatoes to the sauce. Simmer for an additional 2–3 minutes. Season to taste.

5 Drain the pasta well and stir in the sauce. Toss together until thoroughly combined. Serve immediately.

Seafood Lasagne

Serves 4

INGREDIENTS

¼ cup butter	1 tbsp. fresh thyme leaves	4–6 sheets fresh lasagna
6 tbsp. flour	3 cups mixed mushrooms, sliced	8 oz. mozzarella, drained
1 tsp. mustard powder	⅔ cup white wine	and chopped
2½ cups milk	14 oz. can chopped tomatoes	salt and pepper
2 tbsp. olive oil	1 lb. mixed skinless white fish	
1 onion, chopped	fillets, cubed	
2 garlic cloves, finely chopped	8 oz. fresh scallops, trimmed	

1 Melt the butter in a saucepan. Add the flour and mustard powder and stir until smooth. Simmer gently for 2 minutes without coloring. Gradually add the milk, whisking until smooth. Bring to a boil and simmer for 2 minutes. Remove from the heat and set aside. Cover the surface of the sauce with plastic wrap to prevent a skin forming.

2 Heat the oil in a frying pan and add the onion, garlic, and thyme. Cook gently for 5 minutes until softened. Add the mushrooms and fry for an additional 5 minutes until softened. Stir in the wine and boil rapidly until nearly evaporated. Stir in the tomatoes. Bring to a boil and simmer, covered, for 15 minutes. Season and set aside.

3 Lightly grease a lasagna dish. Spoon half the tomato sauce over the base of the dish and top with half the fish and scallops.

4 Layer half the lasagna over the fish, pour over half the white sauce, add half the mozzarella. Repeat these layers, finishing with the white sauce and mozzarella.

5 Bake in a preheated oven at 400° F for 35–40 minutes until bubbling and golden and the fish is cooked through. Remove from the oven and leave to stand on a heat resistant surface or mat for 10 minutes before serving.

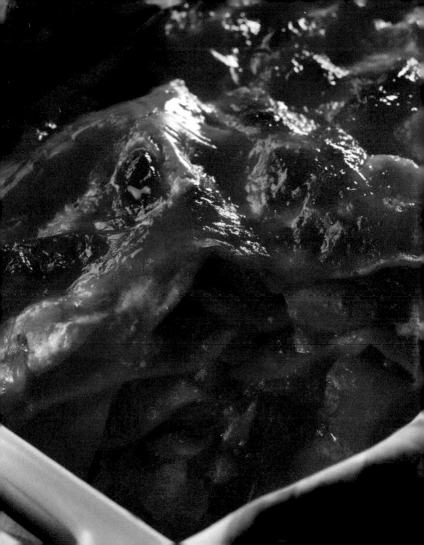

Spaghetti al Vongole

Serves 4

INGREDIENTS

2 lb. live clams, scrubbed
2 tbsp. olive oil
1 large onion, finely chopped
2 garlic cloves, finely chopped

1 tsp. fresh thyme leaves
⅔ cup white wine
14 oz. can chopped tomatoes
12 oz. dried spaghetti

1 tbsp. chopped fresh parsley
salt and pepper

1 Put the clams into a large saucepan with just the water clinging to their shells. Cook, covered, over a high heat for 3–4 minutes, shaking the pan occasionally, until all the clams have opened. Remove from the heat and strain, reserving the cooking liquid. Discard any clams that remain closed. Set aside.

2 Heat the oil in a saucepan and add the onion. Cook for 10 minutes over a low heat until softened but not colored. Add the garlic and thyme

and cook for an additional 30 seconds. Increase the heat and add the white wine. Simmer rapidly until reduced and syrupy. Add the tomatoes and reserved clam cooking liquid. Cover and simmer for 15 minutes. Uncover and simmer for an additional 15 minutes until thickened. Season to taste.

3 Meanwhile, cook the spaghetti in plenty of boiling salted water according to the packet instructions, until tender but still firm to the bite. Drain well and return to the pan.

4 Add the clams to the tomato sauce and heat through for 2–3 minutes. Add the parsley and stir well. Add the tomato sauce to the pasta and toss together until the pasta is well coated in sauce. Serve immediately.

COOK'S TIP

If you are only able to get very large clams, reserve a few in their shells to garnish and shell the rest.

Linguini with Sardines

Serves 4

INGREDIENTS

8 sardines, filleted	1 tsp. chili flakes	2 tbsp. pine nuts, toasted
1 bulb fennel	12 oz. dried linguine	2 tbsp. chopped fresh parsley
4 tbsp. olive oil	½ tsp. finely grated lemon rind	salt and pepper
3 garlic cloves, sliced	1 tbsp. lemon juice	

1 Wash and dry the sardine fillets. Roughly chop into large pieces and set aside. Trim the fennel bulb and slice very thinly.

2 Heat 2 tablespoons of the olive oil in a large frying pan and add the garlic and chili flakes. Cook for 1 minute then add the fennel. Cook over a medium high heat for 4–5 minutes until softened. Add the sardine pieces and cook for an additional 3–4 minutes until just cooked.

3 Meanwhile, cook the pasta in plenty of boiling salted water according to the package instructions, until tender but still firm to the bite. Drain well and return to the pan.

4 Add the lemon rind, lemon juice, pine nuts, parsley, and seasonings to the sardines and toss together. Add to the pasta with the remaining olive oil and toss together gently. Serve immediately while the pasta is still hot with a sprinkling of parsley.

COOK'S TIP

Reserve a couple of tablespoons of the pasta cooking water and add to the pasta with the sauce if the mixture seems a little dry.

Crab Ravioli

Serves 4

INGREDIENTS

2 cups all-purpose flour, or
    type "00" Italian pasta flour
1 tsp. salt
2 eggs plus 1 egg yolk
1 tbsp. olive oil
8 oz. raw shrimp, finely chopped
8 oz. white crab meat
1 tbsp. chopped fresh chervil
1 tbsp. chopped fresh chives

1 tbsp. chopped fresh parsley
1 tsp. grated rind lime
4 tbsp. heavy cream
salt and pepper

RED BELL PEPPER SAUCE
½ large red bell pepper, cored,
    deseeded and halved
1 tsp. olive oil, for brushing

¼ cup unsalted butter, softened
1 tbsp. lime juice
salt and pepper

TO GARNISH
lime wedges
fresh chives

1 To make the pepper sauce, brush the pepper pieces with the olive oil. Place under a preheated hot broiler for 3–4 minutes on each side until charred and tender. Remove from the heat and place in a plastic bag until cool enough to handle. Discard the skin and put in a food processor or blender. Add the butter, lime juice and seasoning and blend until smooth. Set aside.

2 To make the pasta, sift the flour and salt into a bowl. Make a well in the center and add the eggs, egg yolk, oil, and enough water to make a firm dough. Knead for 5 minutes. Wrap in plastic wrap and chill.

3 Meanwhile, mix together the shrimp, crab, chervil, chives, parsley, lime rind, cream, and seasoning and set aside.

4 Divide the pasta dough into 8 pieces. Using a pasta machine, roll out each piece as thinly as possible. Dust the surface liberally with flour and top with 1 sheet of pasta. Place a teaspoon of filling at 1 inch intervals along the dough. Brush lightly around the filling

with water then place a second sheet of pasta on top.

5 Press down firmly around each mound of filling to seal then, using a pastry cutter or pasta wheel, cut out the ravioli. Repeat with the remaining pasta and filling, placing the cut out ravioli on a well-floured dishtowel.

6 Bring a large saucepan of lightly salted water to a boil and add the ravioli. Boil for 3–4 minutes until the pasta is tender but still firm to the bite. Drain well and toss immediately with the pepper sauce. Serve immediately, while the ravioli is still hot garnished with lime wedges and snipped fresh chives.

Spaghettini with Crab

Serves 4

INGREDIENTS

1 dressed crab, about 1 lb.
including the shell
12 oz. dried spaghettini
6 tbsp. best quality extra-virgin
olive oil

1 hot red chili, deseeded and
finely chopped
2 garlic cloves, finely chopped
3 tbsp. chopped fresh parsley
1 tsp. finely grated lemon juice

2 tbsp. lemon juice
salt and pepper
lemon wedges, to garnish

1 Scoop the meat from the crab shell into a bowl. Mix the white and brown meat lightly together and set aside.

2 Bring a large saucepan of salted water to a boil and add the spaghettini. Cook according to the instructions on the packet until tender but still firm to the bite. Drain well and return to the pan.

3 Meanwhile, heat 2 tablespoons of the olive oil in a frying pan.

When hot, add the chili and garlic. Cook for 30 seconds before adding the crab meat, parsley, lemon juice, and lemon rind. Stir-fry for an additional minute until the crab is just heated through.

4 Add the crab mixture to the pasta with the remaining olive oil and seasoning. Toss together thoroughly and serve immediately, garnished with lemon wedges.

COOK'S TIP

If you prefer to buy your own fresh crab you will need a large crab weighing about 2 lb. 4 oz.

Squid Ink Pasta

Serves 4

INGREDIENTS

1 lb. squid with their ink	SAUCE	3 plum tomatoes, peeled,
2½ cups all-purpose flour or	4 tbsp. olive oil	deseeded and diced
type "00" Italian pasta flour	2 garlic cloves, finely chopped	⅔ cup white wine
3½ oz. fine semolina	1 tsp. paprika	1 tbsp. chopped fresh parsley
2 eggs		salt and pepper

1 To prepare the squid and its ink, carefully grasp the head and tentacles of the squid and pull to remove all the innards. The ink sack lies at the furthest point from the tentacles and is a silverish tube—be careful to keep it intact. Cut the ink sack away from the innards and set aside. Cut the tentacles just below the beak and discard the remaining innards. Remove the stiff cartilage from the body and remove the wings and skin. Wash the body and tentacles well.

2 Slice the body widthwise into rings and set aside

with the tentacles. Slit open the ink sack and dilute with water to make about ¼ cup. Set aside.

3 To make the pasta, sift together the flour and semolina. Make a well in the center and add the eggs. Using a wooden spoon, draw the flour and eggs together. Gradually add the squid ink— you may not need it all. Mix to a firm dough. Add a little more water if it seems too stiff and a little more flour if it seems too wet. Alternatively, put all the ingredients in the bowl of a mixer fitted with a kneading hook and mix together. Knead the dough for 10 minutes until smooth and elastic. The dough should have the feel of soft leather and be neither sticky nor easily broken. Wrap in plastic wrap and set aside for 30 minutes.

4 Using a pasta machine, thinly roll out the dough and cut into thin ribbons. Hang up the pasta to dry.

5 Meanwhile, make the sauce, heat the oil in a saucepan and then add the garlic and paprika. Fry over a medium heat for 30 seconds. Add the squid and, keeping the heat high, cook for 4–5 minutes until lightly browned and firm. Add the tomatoes and cook for 3–4 minutes until collapsed. Add the white wine and simmer gently for 15 minutes. Stir in the parsley and season to taste.

6 Meanwhile, bring a large pan of salted water to the boil and add the pasta. Cook for 2–3 minutes until tender but still firm to the bite then drain thoroughly. Turn the pasta into a large serving bowl, toss together with the sauce and serve immediately.

Fideua

Serves 4

INGREDIENTS

3 tbsp. olive oil
1 large onion, chopped
2 garlic cloves, finely chopped
pinch saffron, crushed
½ tsp. paprika
3 tomatoes, skinned, deseeded
   and chopped

12 oz. egg vermicelli, broken into
   5 cm/2 inch lengths
⅔ cup white wine
1¼ cups fish stock
12 large raw jumbo shrimp
18 live mussels, scrubbed
   and bearded

12 oz. cleaned squid, cut
   into rings
18 large clams, scrubbed
2 tbsp. chopped fresh parsley
salt and pepper
lemon wedges, to serve

1 Heat the oil in a large frying pan or paella pan. Add the onion and cook gently for 5 minutes until softened. Add the garlic and cook for an additional 30 seconds. Add the saffron and paprika and stir well. Add the tomatoes and cook for an additional 2–3 minutes, stirring gently, until they have softened.

2 Add the vermicelli and stir well. Add the wine and boil rapidly until it has been absorbed.

3 Add the fish stock, shrimp, mussels, squid, and clams. Stir and return to a low simmer for about 10 minutes until the shrimp and squid are cooked through and the mussels and clams have opened. The stock should be almost completely absorbed.

4 Add the parsley and season to taste. Serve immediately, in warm bowls, garnished with lemon wedges.

VARIATION

Use whatever combination of seafood you prefer. Try langoustines, shrimp, and monkfish.

Thai Noodles

Serves 4

INGREDIENTS

12 oz. jumbo shrimp,
    cooked and peeled
4 oz. flat rice noodles or
    rice vermicelli
4 tbsp. vegetable oil
2 garlic cloves, finely chopped

1 egg
2 tbsp. lemon juice
1½ tbsp. Thai fish sauce
½ tsp. sugar
2 tbsp. chopped, roasted peanuts
½ tsp. cayenne pepper

2 scallions, cut into 1 inch pieces
1¾ oz. fresh beansprouts
1 tbsp. chopped cilantro
lemon wedges, to serve

1 Drain the shrimp on paper towels to remove excess moisture. Set aside. Cook the rice noodles according to the packet instructions. Drain well and set aside.

2 Heat the oil in a wok or large frying pan and add the garlic. Fry until just golden. Add the egg and stir quickly to break it up. Cook for a few seconds.

3 Add the shrimp and noodles, scraping down the sides of the pan to ensure they mix with the egg and chopped garlic.

4 Add the lemon juice, fish sauce, sugar, half the peanuts, cayenne pepper, the scallions, and half the beansprouts stirring quickly all the time. Cook over a high heat for an additional 2 minutes until everything is heated through.

5 Turn on to a serving plate. Top with the remaining peanuts and beansprouts and sprinkle with the cilantro. Serve with lemon wedges.

VARIATION

This is a basic dish to which lots of different cooked seafood could be added. Cooked squid rings, mussels, and langoustines would all work just as well.

Kedgeree

Serves 4

INGREDIENTS

1 lb. undyed smoked haddock fillet	½ tsp. ground cumin	TO SERVE
2 tbsp. olive oil	1 tsp. ground coriander	lemon wedges
1 large onion, chopped	¾ cup basmati rice	mango chutney
2 garlic cloves, finely chopped	4 medium eggs	
½ tsp. ground turmeric	2 tbsp. butter	
	1 tbsp. chopped fresh parsley	

1 Pour boiling water over the haddock fillet and leave for 10 minutes. Lift the fish from the cooking water, discard the skin and bones, and flake the fish. Set aside. Reserve the cooking water.

2 Heat the oil in a large saucepan and add the onion. Cook for 10 minutes over a medium heat until starting to brown. Add the garlic and cook for an additional 30 seconds. Add the turmeric, cumin, and coriander and stir-fry for 30 seconds until the spices smell fragrant. Add the rice and stir well.

3 Measure 1½ cups of the haddock cooking water and add this to the pan. Stir well and bring to a boil. Cover and cook over a very low heat for 12–15 minutes until the rice is tender and the stock is absorbed.

4 Meanwhile, bring a small saucepan of water to a boil and add the eggs. When the water has returned to a boil cook the eggs for 8 minutes. Immediately drain the eggs and refresh under cold water to stop them cooking. Set aside.

5 Add the reserved fish pieces, the butter and parsley to the rice. Turn on to a large serving dish. Shell and quarter the eggs and arrange on top of the rice. Serve them with lemon wedges and mango chutney.

A Modern Kedgeree

Serves 4

INGREDIENTS

2 tbsp. butter
1 tbsp. olive oil
1 onion, finely chopped
1 garlic clove, finely chopped
¾ cup long-grain rice

1⅔ cups fish stock
6 oz. skinless, boneless salmon
    fillet, chopped
3 oz. smoked salmon, chopped
2 tbsp. heavy cream

2 tbsp. chopped fresh dill
3 scallions, finely chopped
salt and pepper
lemon slices and fresh dill,
    to garnish

1 Melt the butter with the oil in a large saucepan. Add the onion and cook gently for 10 minutes until softened but not colored. Add the garlic and cook for an additional 30 seconds.

2 Add the rice and cook for 2–3 minutes, stirring, until transparent. Add the fish stock and stir well. Bring to a boil, cover and simmer very gently for 10 minutes.

3 Add the salmon fillet and the smoked salmon and stir well, adding a little more stock or water if it seems dry. Return to the heat and cook an additional 6–8 minutes until the fish and rice are tender and all the stock is absorbed.

4 Remove the pan from the heat—or make sure that your stove is turned off—and stir in the cream, dill, and scallions. Season to taste and serve immediately, garnished with a sprig of dill and a slice of lemon.

COOK'S TIP

*Use smoked salmon
trimmings for a
budget dish.*

Jambalaya

Serves 4

INGREDIENTS

2 tbsp. vegetable oil

2 onions, roughly chopped

1 green bell pepper, deseeded and roughly chopped

2 celery stalks, roughly chopped

3 garlic cloves, finely chopped

2 tsp. paprika

10½ oz. skinless, boneless chicken breasts, chopped

3½ oz. boudin sausages, chopped

3 tomatoes, skinned and chopped

2 cups long-grain rice

3¾ cups hot chicken or fish stock

1 tsp. dried oregano

2 fresh bay leaves

12 large jumbo shrimp tails

4 scallions, finely chopped

2 tbsp. chopped fresh parsley

salt and pepper

salad, to serve

1 Heat the vegetable oil in a large frying pan and add the onions, bell pepper, celery, and garlic. Cook for 8–10 minutes until all the vegetables have softened. Add the paprika and cook for an additional 30 seconds. Add the chicken and sausages and cook for 8–10 minutes until lightly browned. Add the tomatoes and cook for 2–3 minutes until softened.

2 Add the rice to the pan and stir well. Pour in the hot stock, oregano, and bay leaves and stir well. Cover and simmer for 10 minutes over a very low heat.

3 Add the shrimp and stir well. Cover again and cook for an additional 6–8 minutes until the rice is tender and the shrimp are cooked through.

4 Stir in the scallions, parsley and season to taste. Serve immediately.

COOK'S TIP

Jambalaya is a dish with many variations— use whatever you have at hand. Boudin is a classic Cajun sausage. Any spicy sausage would also work.

Lobster Risotto

Serves 4

INGREDIENTS

1 cooked lobster, weighing
about 14 oz.–1 lb.
¼ cup butter
1 tbsp. olive oil
1 onion, finely chopped

1 garlic clove, finely chopped
1 tsp. fresh thyme leaves
¾ cup arborio rice
2½ cups hot fish stock
⅔ cup sparkling wine

1 tsp. canned green or pink
peppercorns in brine, drained
and roughly chopped
1 tbsp. chopped fresh parsley

1 To prepare the lobster, remove the claws by twisting. Crack the claws using the back of a large knife and set aside. Split the body lengthwise. Remove and discard the intestinal vein which runs down the tail, the stomach sack, and the spongy looking gills. Remove the meat from the tail and roughly chop. Set aside with the claws.

2 Heat half the butter and the oil in a large frying pan. Add the onion and cook gently for 4–5 minutes until

softened. Add the garlic and cook for 30 seconds. Add the thyme and the rice. Stir well for 1–2 minutes, until the rice is well coated in the butter and oil and begins to look translucent.

3 Keep the stock on a low heat. Increase the heat under the frying pan to medium and begin adding the stock, a ladleful at a time, stirring well between additions. Continue until all the stock has been absorbed. This should take approximately 20–25 minutes.

4 Add the lobster meat and claws. Stir in the sparkling wine, increasing the heat. When the wine is absorbed, remove the pan from the heat and stir in the green or pink peppercorns, remaining butter and parsley. Leave to stand for 1 minute then serve immediately.

VARIATION

For a slightly cheaper version substitute 1 lb. shrimp for the lobster.

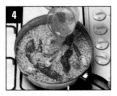

Shrimp & Asparagus Risotto

Serves 4

INGREDIENTS

5 cups vegetable stock
12 oz. asparagus, cut into
　　2 inch lengths
2 tbsp. olive oil
1 onion, finely chopped

1 garlic clove, finely chopped
1½ cups arborio rice
1 lb. raw jumbo shrimp, peeled
　　and de-veined
2 tbsp. olive paste or tapenade

2 tbsp. chopped fresh basil
salt and pepper
Parmesan cheese, to garnish

1 Bring the vegetable stock to a boil in a large saucepan. Add the asparagus and cook for 3 minutes until just tender. Strain, reserving the stock, and refresh the asparagus under cold running water. Drain and set aside.

2 Heat the oil in a large frying pan, add the onion and cook gently for 5 minutes until softened. Add the garlic and cook for an additional 30 seconds.

Add the rice and stir for 1–2 minutes until it is coated with the oil and slightly translucent.

3 Keep the stock on a low heat. Increase the heat under the frying pan to medium and begin adding the stock, a ladleful at a time, stirring well between additions. Continue until almost all the stock has been absorbed. This should take 20–25 minutes.

4 Add the shrimp and asparagus with the last ladleful of stock and cook for an additional 5 minutes until the shrimp and rice are tender and the stock has been absorbed. Remove from the heat.

5 Stir in the olive paste, basil and seasoning and leave to stand for 1 minute. Serve immediately, garnished with Parmesan shavings.

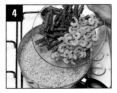

Spicy Coconut Rice with Monkfish & Peas

Serves 4

INGREDIENTS

1 hot red chili, deseeded
    and chopped
1 tsp. crushed chili flakes
2 garlic cloves, chopped
2 pinches saffron
3 tbsp. roughly chopped
    mint leaves

4 tbsp. olive oil
2 tbsp. lemon juice
12 oz. monkfish fillet, cut into
    bite-size pieces
1 onion, finely chopped
2 cups long grain rice
14 oz. can chopped tomatoes

¾ cup coconut milk
4 oz. peas
salt and pepper
2 tbsp. chopped cilantro,
    to garnish

1 In a food processor or blender, blend together the fresh and dried chili, garlic cloves, saffron, mint, olive oil, and lemon juice until finely chopped but not smooth.

2 Put the monkfish pieces into a nonmetallic dish and pour over the spice paste, mixing together well. Set aside for 20 minutes to marinate.

3 Heat a large saucepan until very hot. Using a slotted spoon, lift the monkfish from the marinade and add in batches to the hot pan. Cook for 3–4 minutes until browned and firm. Remove with a slotted spoon and set aside.

4 Add the onion and remaining marinade to the same pan and cook for 5 minutes until softened and lightly browned. Add the rice and stir until well coated. Add the tomatoes and coconut milk. Bring to a boil, cover and simmer very gently for 15 minutes. Stir in the peas, season and arrange the fish over the top. Cover with foil and continue to cook over a very low heat for 5 minutes. Serve garnished with the chopped cilantro.

Fish & Bread Soup

Serves 4

INGREDIENTS

4 lb. mixed whole fish
8 oz. raw shrimp, shell on
10 cups water
²⁄₃ cup olive oil
2 large onions, roughly chopped
2 celery stalks, roughly chopped
1 leek, roughly chopped
1 small fennel bulb, roughly
   chopped
5 garlic cloves, chopped
1 strip orange peel

3 tbsp. orange juice
14 oz. can chopped tomatoes
1 red bell pepper, deseeded
   and sliced
1 bay leaf
1 sprig fresh thyme
large pinch saffron
large pinch cayenne pepper
6–8 thick slices sourdough bread
salt and pepper

RED BELL PEPPER AND
   SAFFRON SAUCE
1 red bell pepper, deseeded
   and quartered
1 egg yolk
large pinch saffron
pinch chili flakes
²⁄₃ cup olive oil
lemon juice, if necessary
salt and pepper

1 Fillet the fish, reserving all the bones. Roughly chop the flesh. Peel the shrimp. Place the fish bones and the shells in a large saucepan with the water and bring to a boil. Simmer for 20 minutes; strain.

2 Heat the oil in a large pan and add the onions, celery, leek, fennel, and garlic. Cook gently for 20 minutes without coloring. Add the orange peel and juice, tomatoes, red bell pepper, bay leaf, thyme, saffron, shrimp, and fish fillets and stock, bring to a boil and simmer for 40 minutes.

3 To prepare the sauce. Brush the red bell pepper quarters with some of the olive oil. Place under a hot preheated broiler for 8–10 minutes, turning once, until the skins have blackened and the flesh is tender. Put in a plastic bag.

4 Once cool, peel off the skin. Roughly chop the flesh and place in a food processor with the egg yolk, saffron, chili flakes, and seasoning. Blend until the red bell pepper is smooth. Add the olive oil, in a slow stream, until the sauce begins to thicken. Continue adding in a steady stream. Add seasoning to taste and lemon juice if required.

5 When the soup is cooked, put in a food processor or blender, blend until smooth and push through a sieve with a wooden spoon. Return to the heat and season with cayenne, salt and pepper to taste.

6 Toast the bread on both sides and place in the bottom of soup plates. Ladle over the soup and serve with the sauce.

Herring & Potato Pie

Serves 4

INGREDIENTS

1 tbsp. Dijon mustard	1 large onion, sliced	1 cup crustless ciabatta
½ cup butter, softened	1 tsp. chopped fresh sage	bread crumbs
1 lb. herrings, filleted	2½ cups hot fish stock (to come	salt and pepper
1 lb. 10 oz. potatoes	halfway up the sides of	parsley sprigs, to garnish
2 cooking apples, sliced thinly	the dish)	

1 Mix the mustard with 2 tablespoons of the butter until smooth. Spread this mixture over the cut sides of the herring fillets. Season and roll up the fillets. Set aside. Generously grease a 9 inch pie pan with some of the remaining butter.

2 Thinly slice the potatoes, using a mandolin if possible. Blanch for 3 minutes in plenty of boiling, salted water until just tender. Drain well, refresh under cold water and pat dry.

3 Heat 2 tablespoons of the remaining butter in a frying pan and add the onion. Cook gently for 8–10 minutes until softened but not colored. Remove from the heat and set aside.

4 Put half the potato slices into the bottom of the pie dish with some seasoning then add half the apple and half the onion. Put the herring fillets on top of the onion and sprinkle with the sage. Repeat the layers in reverse order, ending with potato. Season well and add the hot stock.

5 Melt the remaining butter and stir in the breadcrumbs until well combined. Sprinkle the bread crumbs over the pie. Bake in a preheated oven, at 375° F for 40–50 minutes until the breadcrumbs are golden and the herrings are cooked through. Serve garnished with parsley.

VARIATION

If herrings are unavailable, substitute mackerel or sardines.

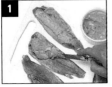

Salt Cod Hash

Serves 4

INGREDIENTS

½ quantity Home-salted Cod
    (see page 90)

4 eggs

3 tbsp. olive oil, plus extra
    for drizzling

8 slices bacon, chopped

1 lb. 9 oz. old potatoes, diced

8 garlic cloves

8 thick slices good-quality
    white bread

2 plum tomatoes, skinned and
    chopped

2 tsp. red wine vinegar

2 tbsp. chopped fresh parsley
    plus extra to garnish

salt and pepper

lemon wedges, to garnish

1 Soak the prepared cod in cold water for 2 hours. Drain well. Bring a large saucepan of water to a boil and add the fish. Remove from the heat and leave to stand for 10 minutes. Drain the fish on paper towels and flake the flesh. Set aside. Discard the soaking water.

2 Bring a saucepan of water to a boil and add the eggs. Simmer for 7–9 minutes from when the water returns to a boil—7 minutes for a slightly soft center, 9 for a firm center.

Immediately drain then plunge the eggs into cold water to stop them cooking further. When cool enough to handle, shell the eggs and roughly chop. Set aside.

3 Heat the oil in a large frying pan and add the bacon. Cook over a medium heat for 4–5 minutes until crisp and brown. Remove with a slotted spoon and drain on paper towel. Add the potatoes to the pan with the garlic and cook over a medium heat for 8–10 minutes until crisp and golden.

4 Toast the bread on both sides until golden. Drizzle with olive oil and set aside.

5 Add the plum tomatoes, bacon, fish, vinegar, and reserved chopped egg to the potatoes and garlic. Cook for an additional 2 minutes. Stir in the parsley and season to taste. Put the toast plates and topped with hash parsley and lemon wedges.

Pizza Marinara

Serves 4

INGREDIENTS

2 cups all-purpose flour
1 tsp. salt
7 g packet easy-blend yeast
2 tbsp. olive oil
²⁄₃ cup hand-hot water

TOMATO SAUCE
2 tbsp. olive oil
1 small onion, finely chopped
1 garlic clove, crushed
14 oz. can chopped tomatoes

1 tsp. dried oregano
1 tbsp. tomato paste
salt and pepper

MIXED SEAFOOD
16 live mussels, scrubbed
    and bearded
16 large clams, scrubbed
1 tbsp. olive oil
12 raw jumbo shrimp
8 oz. cleaned squid, cut into rings

2 x 5½ oz. balls mozzarella,
    drained and sliced
olive oil, for drizzling
handful basil leaves
salt and pepper

1 To make the pizza base, in a large bowl mix together the flour, salt and yeast. Add the oil and enough water to make a soft dough. Knead on a floured surface for 5 minutes until smooth and elastic.

2 Form dough into a neat ball and drop into an oiled bowl. Lightly oil the top of the dough, Cover with a clean dishtowel and leave to rise in a warm place for about 1 hour, or until doubled in bulk.

3 Meanwhile, make the sauce. Heat oil in a pan, add onion and cook for 5 minutes until softened. Add garlic, cook for a few seconds; add tomatoes, oregano, tomato paste, and season. Bring to a boil and simmer, uncovered, for 30 minutes until thick. Leave to cool.

4 Put mussels and clams in a pan with only the water clinging to their shells. Cover and cook over a high heat for 3–4 minutes, shaking occasionally, until the shells have opened. Strain. Discard any that remain closed. When cool enough to handle, remove the seafood from their shells and set aside.

5 Heat the oil in a frying pan and add the shrimp and squid. Cook for 2–3 minutes until the shrimp have turned pink and the squid has become firm. Do not overcook at this stage.

6 Preheat the oven to 450° F, with baking sheets on the top and middle shelves. Knock back the risen dough, divide in two and shape into 10 inch rounds. Put on to floured baking sheets.

7 Spread half the tomato sauce on each pizza and add the seafood. Season and top with the cheese. Drizzle with olive oil and sit the sheets on top of the preheated sheets. Cook for 12–15 minutes, swapping halfway through the cooking time, until golden. Serve immediately, sprinkled with the basil.

Onion & Tuna Tart

Serves 4

INGREDIENTS

8 oz. all-purpose flour
1 tsp. salt
7 g packet easy-blend yeast
2 tbsp. olive oil
²/₃ cup hand-hot water

TOPPING
¼ cup butter
2 tbsp. olive oil
9 oz. onions, finely sliced
1 tsp. sugar
1 tsp. salt

1 tsp. fresh thyme leaves
7 oz. can tuna, drained
¼ cup pitted black olives
pepper, to taste
green salad, to serve

1 To make the topping, heat the butter and oil in a large saucepan and add the onions. Stir well and cook, covered, over a very low heat for 20 minutes. Add the sugar and salt. Cook, covered, over the lowest heat for an additional 30–40 minutes, stirring until collapsed and beginning to brown. Uncover and cook an additional 10–15 minutes until evenly golden. Remove from the heat, stir in the thyme and seasoning.

2 Meanwhile, make the base. In a large bowl, mix together the flour, salt and yeast. Add the oil and enough water to make a soft dough that leaves the sides of the bowl clean. Tip the dough on to a lightly floured surface; knead for 5 minutes until smooth and elastic.

Alternatively, use a food mixer with a dough hook and knead for 5 minutes.

3 Form the dough into a neat ball and drop into a lightly oiled bowl. Lightly oil the top of the dough, cover with a clean dishtowel and set aside to rise in a warm place for about 1 hour, or until doubled in bulk.

4 Preheat the oven to 450° F with a baking sheet on the top shelf. Knock back the risen dough by punching down the center with your

fist. Place on the work surface and knead briefly. Roll out the dough to fit a lightly oiled Swiss roll pan measuring 13 x 9 inches, leaving a rim. You may have to stretch the springy dough to fit the pan.

5 Spread the onions in an even layer over the dough. Flake the tuna over the top. Arrange the olives over the tuna and season with black pepper. Transfer the tin to the preheated baking sheet and cook for 20 minutes until the dough is golden. Serve immediately, with green salad.

Fish Pasties

Serves 4

INGREDIENTS

4 cups self-rising flour	3 oz. leek, diced	4 tsp. white wine vinegar
pinch salt	3 oz. onion, finely chopped	1 oz. cheddar cheese, grated
1¼ cups butter, diced	3 oz. carrot, diced	1 tsp. chopped fresh tarragon
1 egg, lightly beaten	8 oz. potato, diced	salt and pepper
	12 oz. firm white fish (use the	
FILLING	cheapest available), cut	TO SERVE
¼ cup butter	into 1 inch pieces	mixed salad leaves and tomatoes

1 In a large bowl, sift together the flour and salt. Add the butter and rub in with your fingertips until the mixture resembles coarse breadcrumbs. Add about 3 tablespoons cold water to form a dough. Knead the dough briefly until smooth then cover with plastic wrap and chill for 30 minutes.

2 To make the filling, melt half the butter in a large frying pan and add the leek, onion, and carrot. Cook gently for 7–8 minutes until the vegetables are softened.

Remove from the heat, put to one side and allow the mixture to cool slightly.

3 Put the vegetable mixture into a large mixing bowl and add the potato, fish, vinegar, remaining butter, cheese, tarragon, and seasoning. Set aside.

4 Remove the pastry from the refrigerator and roll out thinly. Using a pastry cutter, press out four 7½ inch disks. Alternatively, use a small plate of a similar size. Divide the filling between the

4 disks. Moisten the edges of the pastry and fold over. Pinch to seal. Crimp the edges and place the pasties on a lightly greased baking sheet. Brush generously with the beaten egg, avoiding the base of the pastry to prevent the pasties sticking to it.

5 Bake in a preheated oven at 400° F for 15 minutes. Remove from the oven and brush again with the egg glaze. Return to the oven for an additional 20 minutes. Serve hot or cold with a salad of mixed leaves and tomatoes.

Buckwheat Pancakes with Smoked Salmon & Crème Fraîche

Serves 4

INGREDIENTS

½ cup all-purpose flour
½ cup buckwheat flour
pinch salt
2 large eggs
¾ cup milk
scant ½ cup water
2 tbsp. butter, melted
vegetable oil for frying

FILLING
½ cup crème fraîche
1 tbsp. capers, drained, rinsed
    and roughly chopped
3 scallions, finely chopped
1 red chili, deseeded and
    finely chopped
1 tbsp. chopped fresh dill

1 tbsp. chopped fresh chives
1 tsp. lemon rind
8 oz. sliced smoked salmon
salt and pepper

1 For the filling, mix together the crème fraiche, capers, scallions, red chili, dill, chives, lemon rind, and seasoning and set aside.

2 To make the buckwheat pancakes, sift together the flours and salt into a large bowl. Make a well in the center and add the eggs. Mix together the milk and water and add half this mixture to the flour and eggs. Mix together until

smooth. Gradually add the remaining milk until you have a smooth batter. Stir in the melted butter.

3 Heat an 8 inch frying pan over a medium heat. Dip a piece of wadded paper towel into a little vegetable oil and rub this over the surface of the pan to give a thin coating. Ladle about 2 tablespoons pancake mixture to the pan, tilting and shaking the pan to coat

the bottom evenly. Cook for 1 minute until the edges start to lift away from the pan. Using a large palette knife, carefully lift the pancake and turn it over. It should be pale golden. Cook for 30 seconds on the second side. Remove from the pan and place on a warmed plate. Re-grease and reheat the pan and repeat with the remaining mixture to make 12–14 pancakes, depending on their thickness.

4 Place a slice of smoked salmon on each pancake and top with almost 2 teaspoons of the crème fraîche mixture. Fold the pancake in half and then in half again to form a triangle.

Entertaining

The recipes in this chapter have been designed for those occasions when you really want to make an impression. Fish and shellfish are ideal for entertaining.

They are perceived to be more exotic than many meat dishes and yet are often easier to prepare. Shellfish in particular is thought to be luxurious, but nowadays it is readily available and reasonably priced.

There should be something here for every budget, ability, and taste, from Stuffed Monkfish Tail and Crab Soufflé to Hot-smoked Trout Tart and Spinach Roulade.

There are more traditional dishes, such as Luxury Fish Pie and Sole Florentine as well as more exciting dishes like Cuttlefish in their own Ink.

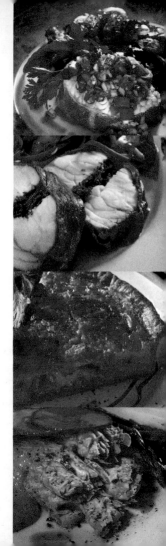

Skate with Black Butter

Serves 4

INGREDIENTS

2 lb. skate wings, cut into 4
¾ cup butter
¾ cup red wine vinegar
½ oz. capers, drained
1 tbsp. chopped fresh parsley
salt and pepper

COURT-BOUILLON
3¾ cups cold water
3¾ cups dry white wine
3 tbsp. white wine vinegar
2 large carrots, roughly chopped
1 onion, roughly chopped
2 celery sticks, roughly chopped
2 leeks, roughly chopped
2 garlic cloves, roughly chopped
2 fresh bay leaves

4 parsley sprigs
4 thyme sprigs
6 black peppercorns
1 tsp. salt

TO SERVE
new potatoes
green vegetable

1 Begin by making the court-bouillon. Put all of the ingredients into a large saucepan and bring slowly to a boil. Cover and simmer gently for 30 minutes. Strain the liquid through a fine sieve into a clean pan. Bring to a boil again and simmer fast, uncovered, for 15–20 minutes, until reduced to 2½ cups.

2 Place the skate in a wide shallow pan and pour over the court-bouillon. Bring to a boil and simmer very gently for 15 minutes, or a little longer depending on the thickness of the skate. Drain the fish and put to one side, keeping warm.

3 Meanwhile, melt the butter in a frying pan. Cook over a medium heat until the butter changes color to a dark brown and smells very nutty.

4 Add the vinegar, capers and parsley and allow to simmer for 1 minute. Pour over the fish. Serve immediately with plenty of boiled new potatoes and a any seasonal fresh green vegetable of your choice.

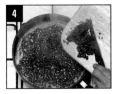

Dover Sole à la Meunière

Serves 4

INGREDIENTS

½ cup all-purpose flour	⅔ cup butter	¼ preserved lemon, finely
1 tsp. salt	3 tbsp. lemon juice	chopped (optional)
4 x 14 oz. Dover soles, cleaned	1 tbsp. chopped fresh parsley	salt and pepper
and skinned		lemon wedges, to garnish

1 Mix the flour with the salt and place on a large plate or tray. Drop the fish into the flour, one at a time, and shake to remove any excess. Melt 3 tablespoons of the butter in a small saucepan and use to liberally brush the Dover soles all over.

2 Place the fish under a preheated hot broiler and cook for 5 minutes each side.

3 Meanwhile, melt the remaining butter in pan. Pour cold water into a bowl, large enough to take the base of the pan. Keep nearby.

4 Heat the butter until it turns a golden brown and begins to smell nutty. Remove immediately from the heat and immerse the base of the pan in the cold water, to arrest cooking.

5 Put the fish on to individual serving plates, drizzle with the lemon juice and sprinkle with the parsley and preserved lemon, if using. Pour over the browned butter and serve immediately, garnished with lemon wedges.

COOK'S TIP

If you have a large enough pan (or two) you can fry the floured fish in butter, if you prefer.

Sole Florentine

Serves 4

INGREDIENTS

2½ cups milk

2 strips lemon rind

2 sprigs fresh tarragon

1 fresh bay leaf

½ onion, sliced

2 tbsp. butter

½ cup all-purpose flour

2 tsp. mustard powder

3 tbsp. freshly grated
Parmesan cheese

2¼ cups heavy cream

pinch freshly grated nutmeg

1 lb. fresh spinach, washed

4 x 1 lb. 10 oz. Dover sole,
quarter-cut fillets (two from
each side of the fish)

salt and pepper

TO SERVE

crisp green salad

crusty bread

1 Put the milk, lemon rind, tarragon, bay leaf, and onion into a saucepan and bring slowly to a boil. Remove from the heat and set aside for 30 minutes for the flavors to infuse.

2 Melt the butter in a clean saucepan and stir in the flour and mustard powder until smooth. Strain the infused milk, discarding the lemon, herbs, and onion. Gradually beat the milk into the butter and flour until smooth. Bring slowly to a boil, stirring constantly, until thickened. Simmer gently for 2 minutes. Remove from the heat and stir in the cheese, heavy cream, nutmeg, and seasoning. Cover the surface of the sauce with baking parchment or plastic wrap and set aside.

3 Lightly grease a large baking dish. Blanch the spinach leaves in plenty of boiling salted water for 30 seconds. Drain and immediately refresh under cold water. Drain and pat dry.

Arrange the spinach in a layer on the bottom of the greased baking dish.

4 Wash and dry the fish fillets. Season and roll up. Arrange on top of the spinach and pour over the cheese sauce. Transfer to a preheated oven at 400°F and cook for 35 minutes until bubbling and golden. Serve immediately with a crisp green salad and crusty bread.

VARIATION

*For a budget version
of this dish, use lemon
sole instead of
Dover sole.*

John Dory en Papillote

Serves 4

INGREDIENTS

2 John Dory, filleted
1 cup pitted black olives
12 cherry tomatoes, halved
4 oz. green beans, trimmed

handful fresh basil leaves
4 slices fresh lemon
4 tsp. olive oil
salt and pepper

fresh basil leaves, to garnish
boiled new potatoes, to serve

1 Wash and dry the fish fillets and set aside. Cut 4 large rectangles of baking parchment measuring about 18 x 12 inches. Fold in half to make a 9 x 12 inch rectangle. Cut this into a large heart shape and open out.

2 Lay one John Dory fillet on one half of the paper heart. Top with a quarter of the olives, tomatoes, green beans, basil, and one lemon slice. Drizzle over 1 teaspoon of olive oil and season well with salt and pepper.

3 Fold over the other half of the paper and fold the edges of the paper together to enclose. Repeat to make 4 packets.

4 Place the packets on a baking sheet and cook in a preheated oven at 400° F, for 15 minutes or until the fish is tender.

5 Transfer each parcel to a serving plate, unopened, allowing your guests to open their packets and enjoy the wonderful aroma. Suggest that they garnish their portions with fresh basil and serve with a generous helping of boiled new potatoes.

VARIATION

Try spreading the fish with a little olive paste, some chopped sun-dried tomatoes, a little goat cheese, and fresh basil.

Grilled Sea Bass with Stewed Artichokes

Serves 4

INGREDIENTS

4 lb. baby artichokes

2½ tbsp. fresh lemon juice, plus the cut halves of the lemon

⅔ cup olive oil

10 garlic cloves, finely sliced

1 tbsp. fresh thyme, plus extra to garnish

6 x 4 oz. sea bass fillets

1 tbsp. olive oil

salt and pepper

crusty bread, to serve

1 Peel away the tough outer leaves of each artichoke until the yellow-green heart is revealed. Slice off the pointed top at about halfway between the point and the top of the stem. Cut off the stem and pare off what is left of the dark green leaves surrounding the bottom of the artichoke.

2 Submerge the prepared artichokes in water containing the cut halves of the lemon to prevent them browning. When all the artichokes have been prepared, turn them, choke side down, and slice thinly.

3 Warm the olive oil in a large saucepan and add the sliced artichokes, garlic, thyme, lemon juice and seasoning. Cover and cook the artichokes over a low heat for 20–30 minutes, without coloring, until tender.

4 Meanwhile, brush the sea bass fillets with the remaining olive oil and season well. Cook on a preheated ridged griddle or barbecue for 3–4 minutes on each side until just tender.

5 Divide the stewed artichokes between serving plates and top each with a sea bass fillet. Garnish with chopped thyme and serve with lots of crusty bread.

VARIATION

Artichokes cooked this way also suit cod, halibut, or salmon.

Sea Bass with Ratatouille

Serves 4

INGREDIENTS

2 large sea bass, filleted
olive oil, for brushing
salt and pepper

RATATOUILLE
1 large eggplant
2 medium zucchini
1 tbsp. sea salt
4 tbsp. olive oil

1 medium onion, peeled and
    roughly chopped
2 garlic cloves, crushed
½ red bell pepper, deseeded and
    roughly chopped
½ green bell pepper, deseeded
    and roughly chopped
2 large ripe tomatoes, skinned
    and chopped
1 tbsp. freshly chopped basil

DRESSING
5 tbsp. roughly chopped
    fresh basil
2 garlic cloves, roughly chopped
4 tbsp. olive oil
1 tbsp. lemon juice
salt and pepper

1 To make the ratatouille, cut the eggplant and zucchini into chunks about the same size as the onion and bell peppers. Put the eggplant and zucchini in a colander with the salt and set aside to drain for 30 minutes. Rinse thoroughly and pat dry on paper towels. Set aside.

2 Heat the oil in a large saucepan and add the onion and garlic. Cook gently for 10 minutes until softened. Add the bell peppers, eggplant, and zucchini. Season and stir well. Cover and simmer very gently for 30 minutes until all the vegetables have softened. Add the tomatoes and cook for an additional 15 minutes.

3 Meanwhile make the dressing. Put the basil, garlic, and half the olive oil into a food processor and blend until finely chopped. Add the remaining olive oil, lemon juice and seasoning.

4 Season the sea bass fillets and brush with a little oil. Preheat a frying pan until very hot and add the fish, skin side down. Cook for 2–3 minutes until the skin is browned and crispy. Turn the fish and cook for an additional 2–3 minutes until just cooked through.

5 To serve, stir the basil into the ratatouille then divide between 4 serving plates. Top with the fresh fried fish and spoon around the dressing.

Whole Sea Bass with Ginger & Scallions

Serves 4

INGREDIENTS

1 lb. 12 oz. whole sea bass,
    cleaned and scaled
4 tbsp. light soy sauce
5 scallions, cut into long,
    fine shreds

2 tbsp. finely shredded
    fresh ginger
4 tbsp. cilantro leaves
5 tsp. sunflower oil
1 tsp. sesame oil

4 tbsp. hot fish stock
steamed rice, to serve
lime wedges, to garnish

1 Wash the fish and pat it dry, then brush with 2 tablespoons of the soy sauce. Scatter half the scallions and all the ginger over a steaming tray or large plate and put the fish on top.

2 Half fill a large saucepan with water and fit a steamer on top. Bring the water to a boil. Put the steaming plate with the sea bass into the steamer and cover with a tight-fitting lid. Keeping the water boiling, steam the fish for about 10–12 minutes until tender.

3 Carefully remove the plate and lift the fish on to a serving platter, leaving behind the scallions and ginger. Scatter over the remaining scallions and the cilantro leaves.

4 Put the sunflower oil into a small saucepan and heat until almost smoking. Add the sesame oil and immediately pour over the fish and scallions. Mix the remaining soy sauce with the fish stock and pour this over the fish. Serve immediately with steamed rice and garnish with the lime wedges.

Cold Poached Cod Steaks with a Pickled Vegetable Relish

Serves 4

INGREDIENTS

1 small carrot, thinly sliced	PICKLED VEGETABLE RELISH	1 tbsp. capers, drained and rinsed
1 small onion, thinly sliced	1 small carrot, finely diced	2 salted anchovies, soaked in
1 celery stick, thinly sliced	¼ red bell pepper, deseeded and	several changes of water for
3 sprigs fresh parsley	finely diced	15 minutes, chopped
3 sprigs fresh thyme	½ small red onion, finely diced	1 tbsp. red wine vinegar
1 garlic clove, sliced	1 garlic clove, finely chopped	scant ½ cup olive oil
7½ cups water	3 tbsp. finely diced cornichon	2 tbsp. chopped fresh parsley
1 tsp. salt	pickles	salt and pepper
4 x 6 oz. cod steaks	4 tbsp. chopped pitted	salad leaves, to serve
	green olives	

1 Put the carrot, onion, celery, parsley, thyme, garlic, water, and salt into a large saucepan. Bring to a boil and simmer gently for 10 minutes.

2 Add the fish and poach for 5–7 minutes until just firm in the center. Remove the fish with a slotted spoon and leave to cool. Refrigerate for 2 hours.

3 Meanwhile, make the pickled vegetable relish. In a nonmetallic bowl, combine the carrot, red bell pepper, red onion, garlic, cornichons, olives, capers, anchovies, vinegar, olive oil, and parsley. Season to taste, adding a little more vinegar or olive oil to taste. Cover and leave to stand in the refrigerator for 1 hour.

4 To serve, place a cold cod steak on each of 4 serving plates. Spoon the relish over the top. Serve immediately with dressed salad leaves.

Sea Bream in a Salt Crust

Serves 4

INGREDIENTS

2 lb. 4 oz. whole sea bream
1 shallot, thinly sliced
2 sprigs fresh parsley
1 sprig fresh tarragon
2 garlic cloves, roughly chopped
4 lb. 8 oz–5 lb. 8 oz. coarse
   sea salt

LEMON BUTTER SAUCE
2 shallots, very finely chopped
4 tbsp. lemon juice
1¼ cold unsalted butter, diced
salt and pepper

TO GARNISH
lemon wedges
fresh herbs

1 Wash and dry the sea bream. Stuff the body cavity with the shallot, parsley, tarragon, and garlic. Set aside.

2 Sprinkle a thick layer of salt into the bottom of a roasting pan large enough to hold the fish, with lots of space round it. Top with the fish then pour the remaining salt over the fish to completely cover it. Sprinkle the water lightly all over the salt. Cook in a preheated oven for 25 minutes 425° F.

3 To make the lemon butter sauce, put the shallots and lemon juice into a saucepan and simmer gently for 5 minutes. Increase the heat until the lemon juice is reduced by half. Reduce the heat and add the butter, piece by piece, whisking constantly, until all the butter is incorporated and the sauce is thick. Season to taste and keep warm.

4 Remove the fish from the oven and allow to stand for 5 minutes before cracking open the salt.

Remove the fish, garnish with lemon wedges and fresh herbs and serve with the lemon butter sauce.

COOK'S TIP

The salt keeps the fish wonderfully moist and tender, but brush away all traces of the crust before serving.

Cuttlefish in their own Ink

Serves 4

INGREDIENTS

1 lb. small cuttlefish, with their ink (or substitute squid)
4 tbsp. olive oil
1 small onion, finely chopped
2 garlic cloves, finely chopped

1 tsp. paprika, preferably Spanish
6 oz. ripe tomatoes, skinned, deseeded and chopped
½ cup red wine
½ cup fish stock

1½ cups instant polenta
3 tbsp. chopped fresh flat-leaf parsley
salt and pepper

1 To prepare the cuttlefish, cut off the tentacles in front of the eyes and remove the beak-like mouth from the center of the tentacles. Cut the head section from the body and discard it. Cut open the body section from top to bottom along the dark colored back. Remove the cuttle bone and the entrails, reserving the ink sack. Skin the body. Chop the flesh roughly and set aside. Split open the ink sack and dilute the ink in a little water. Set aside.

2 Heat the oil in a large saucepan; add the onion. Cook gently for 8–10 minutes until softened and starting to brown. Add the garlic and cook for an additional 30 seconds. Add the reserved cuttlefish and cook for 5 minutes until starting to brown. Add the paprika and stir for an additional 30 seconds before adding the tomatoes. Cook for 2–3 minutes until collapsed.

3 Add the red wine, fish stock, and diluted ink and stir well. Bring to a boil and simmer gently, uncovered, for 25 minutes until the cuttlefish is tender and the sauce has thickened. Season to taste.

4 Meanwhile, cook the polenta according to the packet instructions. When cooked, remove from the heat and stir in the parsley and seasoning.

5 Divide the polenta between serving plates and top with the cuttlefish and its sauce.

Noisettes of Salmon

Serves 4

INGREDIENTS

4 salmon steaks	1 tbsp. chopped fresh parsley	TO SERVE
¼ cup butter, softened	2 tbsp. vegetable oil	new potatoes
1 garlic clove, crushed	4 tomatoes, skinned, deseeded	green vegetables or salad
2 tsp. mustard seeds	and chopped	
2 tbsp. chopped fresh thyme	salt and pepper	

1 Carefully remove the central bone from the salmon steaks and cut them in half. Curl each piece around to form a medallion and tie with string. Blend together the butter, garlic, mustard seeds, thyme, parsley and seasoning and set aside.

2 Heat the oil in a ridged griddle or frying pan and cook the salmon noisettes on both sides, in batches if necessary, until they are brown.
Drain on paper towels and leave to cool.

3 Cut 4 pieces of baking parchment into 12 inch squares. Place 2 salmon noisettes on top of each square and top with a little of the flavored butter and tomato. Draw up the edges of the paper and fold together to enclose the fish. Place on a baking sheet.

4 Cook in a preheated oven at 400° F for 10–15 minutes or until the salmon is cooked through. Serve immediately while still warm with new potatoes and a cooked green vegetable of your choice.

VARIATION

You can make cod steaks into noisettes in the same way. Cook them with butter flavored with chives and basil.

Whole Poached Salmon

Serves 4–6

INGREDIENTS

3 lb. 5 oz. salmon, cleaned and scaled	WATERCRESS MAYONNAISE	1¾ oz. watercress leaves, roughly chopped
3 x quantity court-bouillon (see Poached Rainbow Trout page 122)	1 egg yolk	1 tbsp. chopped fresh basil
½ cucumber, very thinly sliced	1 garlic clove, crushed	1 cup light olive oil
	1 tsp. Dijon mustard	1 scallion, finely chopped
	1 tbsp. lemon juice	salt and pepper

1 Wash and dry the salmon and remove the fins. Place the salmon in a fish kettle or large, heavy-based roasting pan. Pour over the court-bouillon. Bring slowly to a boil and as soon as the liquid comes to a simmer, remove from the heat and leave to go cold.

2 Meanwhile, make the watercress mayonnaise. Put the egg yolk, garlic, mustard, lemon juice, watercress, and basil into a food processor and blend until the herbs are very finely chopped. Begin adding the olive oil, drop by drop, until the mixture begins to thicken. Continue adding the olive oil in a steady stream until it is all incorporated. Scrape the mayonnaise into a bowl and add the scallion and seasoning. Refrigerate until needed.

3 When the salmon is cold, carefully lift it from the poaching liquid and pat dry. Carefully peel away and discard the skin from the rounder, uppermost side, then carefully turn the fish and remove the skin from the flatter, underside. Carefully slide a large knife along the backbone of the fish to remove the flesh in one piece. Turn it over on to your serving platter so that the cut side is up.

4 Remove the bones from the remaining piece of fish. Finally, turn the remaining flesh on top of the first piece to reform the fish. This makes serving much easier. Place the head and tail back on the fish to make it appear whole.

5 Lay the cucumber slices on top of the fish, starting at the tail end, in a pattern resembling scales. Serve with the mayonnaise.

Stuffed Monkfish Tail

Serves 6

INGREDIENTS

1 lb. 10 oz. monkfish tail, skinned
   and trimmed
6 slices prosciutto
4 tbsp. chopped mixed herbs
   such as parsley, chives,
   basil, and sage

1 tsp. finely grated lemon rind
2 tbsp. olive oil
salt and pepper

TO SERVE
shredded stir-fried vegetables
new potatoes

1 Using a sharp knife, carefully cut down each side of the central bone of the monkfish to leave 2 fillets. Wash the fillets and pat them dry with clean paper towels.

2 Lay the prosciutto slices widthwise on a clean work surface so that they overlap slightly. Lay the fish fillets lengthwise on top of the ham so that the two cut sides face each other.

3 Mix together the chopped herbs and lemon rind. Season well.

Pack this mixture onto the cut surface of one monkfish fillet. Press the 2 fillets together and wrap tightly with the prosciutto slices. Secure with string or toothpicks.

4 Heat the olive oil in a large ovenproof frying pan and place the fish in the pan, seam-side down first, and brown the wrapped monkfish tail all over.

5 Cook in a preheated oven, at 400° F, for 25 minutes until golden and the fish is tender. Remove

from the oven and allow to rest for 10 minutes before slicing thickly. Serve with shredded stir-fried vegetables and new potatoes.

COOK'S TIP

It is possible to remove the central bone from a monkfish tail without separating the two fillets completely. This makes it easier to stuff, but takes some practice.

Grilled Lobster with Beurre Blanc

Serves 4

INGREDIENTS

4 x 1lb. live lobsters	1 tbsp. dry white wine	TO GARNISH
2 tbsp. butter	¼ cup water	salt and pepper
	⅔ cup cold unsalted	lemon wedges
BEURRE BLANC	butter, diced	extra sprigs of fresh herbs
1oz. shallots, finely chopped	2 tsp. chopped fresh tarragon	
1tbsp. white wine vinegar	1tbsp. chopped fresh parsley	

1 Put the lobsters into the freezer for about 2 hours then take a very large knife and cleave them in two, lengthwise behind the head. Dot the lobster flesh with the butter. Transfer to a broiler pan and cook, flesh side up, under a preheated very hot broiler for 5–7 minutes until the flesh of the lobster becomes firm and opaque.

2 Meanwhile, put the shallots into a small saucepan with the vinegar, white wine, and water. Bring to a boil and simmer until only 1 tablespoon of liquid remains. Reduce the heat to low and begin adding the butter, one piece at a time, whisking constantly. Add the next piece of butter when the last bit has been incorporated and continue until you've used all the butter and the sauce has thickened.

3 Stir in the tarragon and parsley and season to taste with salt and pepper.

4 Transfer the lobster to 4 serving plates and spoon over the beurre blanc. Garnish with lemon wedges and fresh herbs.

COOK'S TIP

The SPCA has suggested that putting the lobsters in a freezer for 2 hours before cooking them will kill them painlessly but, if you are squeamish about such things, ask your fish supplier to do it for you.

Lobster & Avocado Salad

Serves 4

INGREDIENTS

2 x 14 oz. cooked lobsters	DRESSING
1 large avocado	1 garlic clove, crushed
1 tbsp. lemon juice	1 tsp. Dijon mustard
8 oz. green beans	pinch sugar
4 scallions, thinly sliced	1 tbsp. balsamic vinegar
2 tbsp. chopped fresh chervil	5 tbsp. olive oil
1 tbsp. chopped fresh chives	salt and pepper

1 To prepare the lobsters, cut them in half lengthwise. Remove the intestinal vein which runs down the tail, stomach sack, and any gray beards from the body cavity at the head end of the lobster. Crack the claws and remove the meat—in one piece if possible. Remove the meat from the tail of the lobster. Roughly chop all the meat and set aside.

2 Split the avocado lengthwise and remove the stone. Cut each half in half again and peel away the skin. Cut the avocado into chunks and toss with the lemon juice. Add to the lobster meat.

3 Bring a large pan of salted water to a boil and add the beans. Cook for 3 minutes then drain and immediately refresh under cold water. Drain again and leave to go completely cold. Cut the beans in half then add to the avocado and lobster.

4 Meanwhile, make the dressing by whisking together the garlic, mustard, sugar, vinegar, and seasoning. Gradually add the oil, whisking, until thickened.

5 Add the scallions, chervil, and chives to the lobster and avocado mixture and toss gently together. Drizzle over the dressing and serve immediately.

Platter of Fruit de Mers

Serves 4

INGREDIENTS

36 live mussels, scrubbed
    and bearded
18 live oysters
3 x 1 lb. cooked lobsters
3 x 1 lb. 10 oz. cooked crabs
36 cooked langoustines or shrimp
selection of clams, cockles,
    and scallops
salt and pepper

MAYONNAISE
1 egg yolk
1 tsp. Dijon mustard
1 tbsp. lemon juice
2¼ cups olive oil

SHALLOT VINAIGRETTE
⅔ cup good quality red
    wine vinegar

3 shallots, finely chopped
1 tbsp. olive oil

TO SERVE
seaweed
crushed ice
3 lemons, cut into wedges

1 To prepare the seafood, steam the mussels, clams, and cockles, if using, with just the water on their shells, for 3–4 minutes until just open. Drain and refresh under cold water. If you prefer to serve the oysters lightly cooked, scrub them and put them into a pan with just a splash of water. Cook over a high heat for 3–4 minutes, drain and refresh under cold water. Scallops should be steamed on the half shell until the flesh turns white.

2 To make the mayonnaise, put the egg yolk, mustard, lemon juice, and seasoning into a food processor and blend for 30 seconds until foaming. Begin adding the olive oil, drop by drop, until the mixture begins to thicken. Continue adding the olive oil in a steady stream until it is incorporated. Taste for seasoning and add a little hot water if the mixture seems too thick. Cover and refrigerate until needed.

3 For the shallot vinaigrette, mix together the vinegar, shallots, oil and seasoning. Leave at room temperature for 2 hours before serving.

4 To assemble the platter, place the seaweed on a large tray or platter and top with the crushed ice. Arrange the shellfish and crustaceans with the lemon wedges around the platter, scattering on more crushed ice as you go. Serve the mayonnaise and shallot vinaigrette separately. Don't forget to provide lobster picks, claw crackers, and finger bowls for your guests.

Bouillabaisse

Serves 6–8

INGREDIENTS

5 tbsp. olive oil
2 large onions, finely chopped
1 leek, finely chopped
4 garlic cloves, crushed
½ small fennel bulb,
    finely chopped
5 ripe tomatoes, skinned
    and chopped
1 sprig fresh thyme
2 strips orange rind

6½ cups hot fish stock
4 lb. 8oz. mixed fish, such as
    John Dory, sea bass, bream,
    red mullet, cod, skate, soft
    shell crabs, raw shrimp,
    langoustines, roughly chopped
    into equal-size pieces
    (small shellfish left whole)
12–18 thick slices French bread
salt and pepper

RED BELL PEPPER AND
    SAFFRON SAUCE
1 red bell pepper, deseeded
    and quartered
⅔ cup light olive oil
1 egg yolk
large pinch saffron
pinch chili flakes
lemon juice, to taste

1 Make the red bell pepper and saffron sauce. Brush the red pepper quarters with a little of the olive oil. Place under a preheated hot broiler, cook for 5–6 minutes on each side until charred and tender. Remove from the heat and place in a plastic bag until cool. Peel the skins away.

2 Place the pepper pieces into a food processor with the egg yolk, saffron, chili flakes, lemon juice, and seasoning and process until smooth. Add the remaining olive oil, drop by drop, until the mixture begins to thicken. Continue until it is all incorporated. Add a little hot water if it seems too thick.

3 Heat the olive oil, add the onions, leek, garlic, and fennel and cook for 10–15 minutes until softened and starting to color. Add the tomatoes, thyme, orange rind, and seasoning and fry for an additional 5 minutes until the tomatoes have collapsed.

4 Add the fish stock and bring to a boil. Simmer gently for 10 minutes until the vegetables are tender. Add the fish and simmer for 10 minutes until the fish is tender.

5 When the soup is ready, toast the bread on both sides. Using a slotted spoon, divide the fish between serving plates. Add some of the soup to moisten the stew and serve with the bread. Pass around the red bell pepper and saffron sauce to accompany. Serve the remaining soup separately.

Crab Soufflé

Serves 4–6

INGREDIENTS

¼ cup plus 1 tbsp. butter, plus extra for greasing	¼ cup all-purpose flour	2 tbsp. chopped fresh chives
1 oz. dried breadcrumbs	1 cup milk	pinch cayenne
1 small onion, finely chopped	1¾ oz. Gruyère cheese, grated	salt and pepper
1 garlic clove, crushed	3 eggs, separated	
2 tsp. mustard powder	8 oz. fresh crab meat, thawed if frozen	

1 Generously butter a 5 cup soufflé dish. Add the breadcrumbs and shake around the dish to coat completely, shaking out any excess. Set the dish aside on a baking sheet.

2 Melt the butter in a large saucepan. Add onion and cook gently for 8 minutes until softened but not colored. Add the garlic and cook for an additional minute.

3 Add the mustard powder and flour and cook for 1 minute. Gradually add the milk, stirring constantly, until smooth. Increase the heat slightly and bring slowly to a boil, stirring constantly. Simmer gently for 2 minutes. Remove from the heat and stir in the cheese. Leave to cool slightly.

4 Lightly beat in the egg yolks then fold in the crab meat, chives, cayenne and season generously.

5 In a clean bowl, whisk the egg whites until they hold stiff peaks. Add a large spoonful of the egg whites to the crab mixture and fold together to slacken. Add the remaining egg whites and fold together carefully but thoroughly. Spoon into the prepared dish.

6 Cook the soufflé in a preheated oven at 400°F for 25 minutes until it is well risen and golden. Serve straight from the oven.

Spinach Roulade

Serves 4

INGREDIENTS

8 oz. frozen spinach, thawed
and well drained
2 tbsp. butter
¼ cup all-purpose flour
¾ cup milk
4 eggs, separated
1 tbsp. chopped fresh tarragon

½ tsp. freshly grated nutmeg
olive oil for brushing
salt and pepper

FILLING
12 oz. skinless smoked cod fillet
4 oz. ricotta cheese

1 oz. Parmesan cheese, grated
4 scallions, finely chopped
2 tbsp. freshly chopped chives
1¾ oz. sun-dried tomatoes in
olive oil, drained well and
finely chopped

1 Grease a 13 x 9 inch Swiss roll tin and line with baking parchment. Squeeze the spinach to remove as much liquid as possible. Chop finely and set aside.

2 Melt the butter in a saucepan, add the flour and cook for 30 seconds, stirring. Gradually add the milk until smooth, stirring constantly. Bring slowly to a boil and then simmer for 2 minutes, stirring. Remove from the heat and allow to cool slightly.

3 Stir in the spinach, egg yolks, tarragon, nutmeg, and seasoning. Whisk the egg whites until they hold stiff peaks. Fold a large spoonful into the spinach mixture to slacken it then fold in the remaining egg whites, carefully but thoroughly to avoid losing any volume. Pour the mixture into the prepared tin and smooth the surface.

4 Cook in a preheated oven at 400° F, for 15 minutes until risen and

golden and firm in the center. Turn out immediately on to a clean dishtowel, peel off the baking parchment and roll up from one short end.

5 For the filling, cover the fillet with boiling water and leave for 10 minutes until just tender. Remove the fish and flake carefully, removing any bones, and mix with the ricotta, Parmesan, scallions, chives, sun-dried tomatoes, and seasoning.

6 Unroll the roulade and spread with the cod mixture, leaving a 1 inch border all around. Tightly re-roll the roulade and return to the oven, seam side down, for 20 minutes.

Luxury Fish Pie

Serves 4

INGREDIENTS

½ cup butter

3 shallots, finely chopped

2 cups button mushrooms, cleaned and halved

2 tbsp. dry white wine

2 lb. live mussels, scrubbed and bearded

1 quantity court-bouillon (see Poached Rainbow Trout, page 122)

300 g/10½ oz. monkfish fillet, cut into cubes

300 g/10½ oz. skinless cod fillet, cubed

10½ oz. skinless lemon sole fillet, cubed

4 oz. jumbo shrimp, peeled

¼ cup all-purpose flour

¼ cup heavy cream

POTATO TOPPING

3 lb. 5oz. floury potatoes, cut into chunks

¼ cup butter

2 egg yolks

½ cup milk

pinch freshly grated nutmeg

salt and pepper

fresh parsley, to garnish

1 For the filling melt 1 oz. butter, add shallots, cook for 5 minutes. Add mushrooms, cook for 2 minutes. Add wine, simmer until liquid has evaporated. Transfer to a 6¼ cup shallow ovenproof dish.

2 Cook the mussels (with just the water clinging to their shells), covered, over a high heat for 3–4 minutes until all have opened. Discard any mussels that remain

closed. Reserve the cooking liquid. Remove the mussels from the shells and add to the mushrooms.

3 Boil the court-bouillon and add monkfish. Poach for 2 minutes. Add cod, sole, and shrimp, poach 2 minutes. Add to the mussel mixture.

4 Melt remaining butter, add flour, cook for 2 minutes. Gradually, stir in the liquid from the mussels until smooth and thickened. Add cream and simmer gently for 15 minutes, stirring. Season to taste with salt and pepper and pour over the fish.

5 Boil the potatoes, drain and mash with the butter, egg yolks, milk, nutmeg and seasoning. Pipe or spread over the fish; roughen with a fork.

6 Bake in a preheated oven at 400° F, for 30 minutes until golden and bubbling. Garnish with fresh parsley.

Salmon Coulibiac

Serves 4

INGREDIENTS

⅓ cup long-grain rice	2 tbsp. chopped fresh parsley	QUICK HOLLANDAISE SAUCE
pinch salt	1 tbsp. chopped fresh dill	¾ cup butter
3 eggs	1 lb. salmon fillet, skinned	1 tbsp. wine vinegar
2 tbsp. vegetable oil	and cubed	2 tbsp. lemon juice
1 onion, finely chopped	1 lb. 2 oz. puff pastry	3 egg yolks
1 garlic clove, crushed	beaten egg, to glaze	salt and pepper
1 tsp. finely grated lemon rind		

1 Cook the rice with the pinch of salt in plenty of boiling water for 7–8 minutes until tender. Drain well and set aside. Bring a small saucepan of water to a boil and add the eggs. Cook for 8 minutes from when the water returns to a boil. Drain and refresh under cold water. When cool enough to handle, shell and slice thinly.

2 Heat the oil in a frying pan and add the onion. Cook gently for 5 minutes until softened. Add the garlic

and cook for an additional 30 seconds. Add to the rice with the lemon rind, parsley, dill and salmon.

3 Roll out pastry to a rectangle measuring 16 x 12 inches. Lift pastry on to a lightly greased baking sheet. Spoon half the filling onto one half of the pastry, leaving a border of about ¾ inch. Top with the eggs and filling.

4 Dampen the outside edges of the pastry with a little beaten egg then fold over the remaining pastry. Crimp the edges to seal well. Mark the pastry using a small sharp knife, taking care not to cut through the pastry. Decorate with pastry trimmings and brush with beaten egg.

5 Bake at 400° F, for 30–35 minutes, until risen and golden.

6 Sauce melt the butter in a small saucepan. Bring the wine vinegar and lemon juice to a boil in another saucepan. Meanwhile, put the egg yolks and a pinch of salt in a blender and blend together. With the motor still running, gradually add the hot vinegar and lemon juice. When the butter starts to boil, start to pour this into the machine in a steady stream until all the butter has been added and the sauce has thickened. Season.

7 Keep warm by placing in a bowl over hot water. Serve the pie with a little hollandaise sauce.

Salmon & Zucchini Pie

Serves 4

INGREDIENTS

2 tbsp. olive oil

2 red bell peppers, cored, deseeded and chopped

1 medium onion, finely chopped

2 eggs

8 oz. salmon fillet, skinned and cubed

1 zucchini, sliced

1 tsp. chopped fresh dill

salt and pepper

Chinese garlic, to garnish

PIE DOUGH

3 cups all-purpose flour

½ tsp. salt

¾ cup cold butter, diced

2 egg yolks

beaten egg or milk, to glaze

1 Heat the oil in a saucepan, add the bell peppers, onion and a little seasoning and cook gently for 10–15 minutes, until softened. Transfer to a food processor or blender and blend until smooth or press through a fine sieve.

2 Bring a small saucepan of water to a boil. Add the eggs, cook for 10 minutes from when the water returns to a boil then refresh immediately under cold water. When cool enough to handle, drain and shell.

3 Roughly chop the eggs and add to the pepper purée with the salmon, zucchini, dill, and seasoning. Mix well and set aside.

4 For the dough, put the flour in a bowl with ½ teaspoon salt. Add the butter and rub in with your fingertips until the mixture resembles fine breadcrumbs. Add the egg yolks with enough cold water, about 3–4 tablespoons, to make a firm dough. Turn on to a lightly floured work surface and knead briefly until smooth.

5 Roll out a little over half of the dough and use to line a 9 inch pie plate. Fill with the salmon mixture and dampen the edges with a little water. Roll out the remaining dough and use to cover the pie, pinching the edges to seal. Make a cross or slash in the top of the pie for steam to escape. Re-roll any dough trimmings and cut into fish tails or leaf shapes and use to decorate the edges of the pie, attaching them with a little beaten egg or milk. Brush more egg or milk over the rest of the pie to glaze.

6 Bake in a preheated oven at 400° F for 35–40 minutes until the pie is golden. Serve hot and garnish with Chinese garlic.

Hot-Smoked Trout Tart

Serves 6

INGREDIENTS

1½ cups all-purpose flour
1 tsp. salt
½ cup butter, cut into small pieces
1 egg yolk

FILLING
25 g/1 oz/2 tbsp. butter
1 small onion, finely chopped

1 tsp. green peppercorns in brine, drained and roughly chopped
2 tsp. candied ginger, drained
2 tsp. candied ginger syrup
8 oz. hot-smoked trout fillets, flaked
3 egg yolks
scant ½ cup crème fraîche
scant ½ cup heavy cream

1 tbsp. chopped fresh parsley
1 tbsp. chopped fresh chives
salt and pepper

1 Sift together the flour and salt. Add the butter and rub in well with your fingertips until the mixture resembles coarse breadcrumbs. Add the egg yolk and about 2 tablespoons cold water, to make a firm dough. Knead briefly, wrap in plastic wrap and refrigerate for 30 minutes.

2 Meanwhile, make the filling. Melt the butter in a frying pan and add the onion. Cook gently for 8–10 minutes until softened but not colored. Remove from the heat and stir in the peppercorns, ginger, ginger syrup and flaked trout. Set aside.

3 Remove the pastry from the refrigerator and roll out thinly. Use to line a 9 inch flan pan or dish. Prick the base at regular intervals with a fork. Line the pastry with foil or baking parchment and baking beans. Bake in a preheated oven at 400° F for 12 minutes. Remove the foil or baking parchment and beans and bake for an additional 10 minutes until light golden and dry. Remove from the oven and allow to cool slightly. Reduce the oven temperature to 350° F. Spread the trout mixture over the base of the pastry.

4 Mix together the egg yolks, crème fraîche, cream, parsley, chives, and seasoning. Pour this mixture over the trout mixture to cover. Bake in the preheated oven for 35–40 minutes until just set and golden. Remove from the oven and allow to cool slightly before serving with a mixed green salad or green vegetable.

Smoked Haddock & Spinach Tart

Serves 6

INGREDIENTS

DOUGH
²⁄₃ cup whole-wheat flour
80 g/3 oz/²⁄₃ cup all-purpose flour
pinch salt
½ cup chilled butter, diced

FILLING
12 oz. smoked haddock fillet
²⁄₃ cup plus 2 tbsp. milk
²⁄₃ cup plus 2 tbsp. heavy cream
4 oz. frozen leaf spinach, thawed

3 egg yolks, lightly beaten
3 oz. mature cheddar
    cheese, grated
salt and pepper

1 For the dough, mix the two flours together in a bowl with the salt. Add the butter and rub in until the mixture resembles fine breadcrumbs. Stir in enough cold water, about 2–3 tablespoons, to make a firm dough. Knead briefly until the dough's surface is smooth.

2 Roll out the dough thinly and use to line a 8 inch deep fluted flan pan. Put in the freezer for 15 minutes. Line with foil or baking parchment and baking beans and bake in a preheated oven, at 400° F, for 10–12 minutes. Remove the foil or parchment and beans and bake for another 10 minutes until pale golden and dry. Cool slightly. Reduce oven temperature to 375° F.

3 Filling place haddock in a frying pan, cover with milk and cream. Bring to a boil, cover and remove from heat. Leave for 10 minutes until the haddock is tender.

Remove the fish using a slotted spoon. Strain the cooking liquid into a jug. Skin and flake the fish.

4 Press the spinach in a sieve to remove excess liquid. Arrange in the pastry case with the flaked fish. Add egg yolks and 2 oz. cheese to the fish poaching liquid. Season. Pour into the pastry case. Sprinkle with remaining cheese and bake for 25–30 minutes until the filling is risen, golden and just set.

Index